BETWEEN THE REALMS

*To Cindy —
A true kindred
spirit! Thanks for
sharing the journey!*

BETWEEN THE REALMS

WHAT GHOSTS TEACH US ABOUT LIFE AND DEATH

Boo Newell

Boo Newell

Mountain Arbor
Press
Alpharetta, GA

The author has tried to recreate events, locations, and conversations from his/her memories of them. The author has made every effort to give credit to the source of any images, quotes, or other material contained within and obtain permissions when feasible.

Copyright © 2017 by Boo Newell

All rights reserved. No part of this book may be reproduced or transmitted in any form or by any means, electronic or mechanical, including photocopying, recording, or any information storage and retrieval system, without permission in writing from the author.

ISBN: 978-1-63183-137-9

Library of Congress Control Number: 2017949924

10 9 8 7 6 5 4 3 2   0 8 0 3 1 7

Printed in the United States of America

⊗This paper meets the requirements of ANSI/NISO Z39.48-1992 (Permanence of Paper)

Photography by Beth Sullivan and Boo Newell

*This book is dedicated to my parents.
To Mom, Fay McClendon Newell, whose fun-loving sense of adventure taught me to seize the day. Carpe diem! Ever undaunted by any obstacle, the motto she lives by is "Full steam ahead!" From her example, I have learned one of life's most important lessons: the only limitations we really have are those we impose on ourselves.*

And to Dad (Pop), Herbert Esley Newell, for teaching me that where there's a will, there's a way—you just have to have the imagination and perseverance to find it.

Thanks, Mom and Dad, for always being there for me. Your unwavering, loving support and belief in me, despite my eccentricities, made all the difference!

CONTENTS

Acknowledgments	ix
Introduction	xi
Denizens of Old Decatur Cemetery	1
I Must Stand Firm	29
I'm Still the Master of Redcliffe Plantation	51
Old Cahawba: A True Ghost Town	77
The Gangster in the Gray House	103
The Guardians of Gost Cave	129
The Lighthouse Keeper Who Never Left	151
The Permanent Guests of the Rumble Seat Inn Bed and Breakfast	173
The Woolfolk Massacre Ghosts of Rose Hill Cemetery	201
But He Promised Me!	229
Closing Thoughts	251
Additional Resources	253
Bibliography	257

ACKNOWLEDGMENTS

First off I would like to give a heartfelt thanks to my editor at Mountain Arbor Press for her professionalism throughout the publishing process. It wasn't just a job to her, but something she genuinely cared about. She saw my vision for *Between the Realms* and made it hers. At the same time, she helped me stay objective about the project. For her caring guidance and honest, insightful critique throughout my publishing journey, I shall remain deeply grateful to her.

Thank you, S., for always being there.

I would also like to thank my good friends Peggy Stancil, Lisalyn Jackson, Martha Arrington, and Chris Glass for their patience and support as they accompanied me on my ghostly adventures. They unselfishly took photos, notes, their time, and did anything else needed to help me get the ghosts' stories. Peggy even acted as ghost bait (albeit unknowingly) for the Rumble Seat Inn adventure.

Big, loving thank-yous go to my dear friends David Dean and Beverly Douds for generously sharing their expertise, scholarly research, and time to answer any questions I might have concerning their respective fields of study. They saved me many hours of research by unstintingly offering their own.

I would like to thank Jenny Dawn Castillo for her hospitality during the Rumble Seat Inn investigation. She graciously shared not only her beautiful mansion with me, but also the ghosts who call it home. (And I, like them, absolutely adore her!)

My friend Andrea Robbins, DC, is someone else I would like to thank. She read the first rough drafts for me, honestly critiquing as she went. Despite these rough drafts, she still managed to stay enthusiastic about the book! A hearty soul, indeed!

Now we come to Beth Sullivan. Words fail me at the thought of all she has done to help *Between the Realms* be born. There were the many times she rescued the manuscript when my computer crashed from being in my energy too long. She happens to be very good with technological matters, whereas I am just the opposite—abysmal! She also critiqued the manuscript throughout the many rough drafts I put it through. Trust me, it took patience. And what about all the adventures she accompanied me on to help with photography and to get the ghosts' stories? (All right, she really went for the history. But what matters, though, is that she went!) Because of all this, and much, much more, I want to offer my sincere, heartfelt gratitude to Beth. Without her unfailing belief in me and the book, completing *Between the Realms* would have been a much more tedious, difficult process. Thank you, Beth, for sharing the load; you lightened it considerably. You are truly a boon companion!

A note to my friends in the spirit realms—the ghosts, and those spirits who have crossed over. These are your stories, and I am deeply grateful that you shared them with me. I am a better person because of this.

Last but definitely not least, I want to thank my siblings, Mac, Esley, Tim, and Bliss, for always believing in me and pushing me to finish this book. Not a family gathering went by without them asking, "Have you finished the book? Have you finished the book?"

Now, finally, I can answer, "Yes, it's DONE!"

INTRODUCTION

Dear readers, my name is Boo Newell. Yes, that's really my name! I've been called Boo since I was a three-day-old baby. Go figure! Was this name a portent of things to come in my life? After all, I now have a successful career as a professional psychic medium, paranormal investigator, spiritual counselor, and animal communicator. I also operate the highly rated Decatur Ghost Tour based in Atlanta, Georgia.

Now, you may be doing something else for a living, but no matter—we're kindred spirits. "How so?" you may ask. Why, just by picking up this book you have exhibited a curiosity about the realm of ghosts shared by me and many others. From my years of experience working with clients and talking to students at workshops and lectures, I have come to suspect that our interest in ghosts is driven by something much deeper than mere curiosity. Could our interest really be coming from a yearning for reassurance that there's life still awaiting us after we walk through the door of death?

The existence of ghosts and other spirits offers this reassurance. After all, they—like us—are first and foremost Divine energetic beings. Why would we just go zap, or disappear into some black abyss? Energy can't be destroyed; it only changes form. So it is with ghosts and other spirits—they've just changed from their physical form back into their true, eternal spirit form. Life goes on and on and on!

Now, you may think that I've always been fond of ghosts and understood them. Not so! I grew up fearing them. I cannot remember a time when I wasn't being touched by the Ghost Realm and its denizens. My earliest childhood memories are not of fluffy stuffed animals around my bed at night. No, my earliest memories are of the ghost of the elderly lady who would come out of the closet when the lights went out. I would watch in horror as she floated toward my bed and stood there, looking down at me. If she ever said anything, I never knew it. I was too busy trembling under the covers.

While some children were worried about the "monster" under the bed, I had to worry about the ghost of the one-eyed man who floated outside my bedroom window two stories above the ground. Bobbing up and down, he would glare at me with that one glowing eye. When I told adults about these otherworldly visitors, I got one of three responses: "It's not nice to tell fibs," "Little Boo has night terrors," and/or "Boo has a great imagination. She's going to grow up to be a great writer." Maybe that last one is true, but it didn't help my ghost problem.

One good thing about having this problem, though, was that I always had someone to play with. Have you ever heard of imaginary playmates? Well, I had plenty of them. For some reason, children's ghosts never scared me. Maybe to a child, a fellow child is a child no matter what form they come in . . . the innocence of childhood, you know. As I grew up, my abilities stuck with me, as did the ghosts. There were also other spirits around me, such as loved ones who had crossed over. Yet growing up, they were all ghosts to me—scary.

Now I realize that all spirits are not ghosts. A ghost is a spirit that has trapped itself in an in-between realm of existence before it can move on to the Other Side. There's even an energy difference of spirits trapped in the Ghost

Realm versus those that have crossed over. A ghost, to some degree, always has an air of confusion about it, whereas the spirit that has crossed over will have a much more settled, calmer energy. After all, they have moved on to where the answers they seek are to be found. With answers come peace and understanding. And so it was with me.

In an attempt to understand and control my fears and strong psychic abilities, I studied and read anything I could get my hands on concerning spiritual, metaphysical matters. Finally, I began to understand the journey I was on. (Notice I said "began." Like everyone else, I'm on a continuous journey of learning.) You know the old saying "With knowledge comes understanding; with understanding comes empowerment." How true this is!

I found peace with who I am, and the ghosts and other spirits who sought me out. These other spirits were from the Other Side. They tended to arrive when I was spending time with their loved ones here in the physical realm. Spirits, after all, can sense and hone in on a human with amped-up psychic abilities. I was always happy to do an impromptu reading for them.

As time went on, friends told me, "Boo, you're good at this. Why don't you turn professional?" So I did! That was eighteen years ago, and I've never looked back. In fact, I now look forward to occasional visits from ghostly friends.

Oh, I do look back sometimes just to see how far I've come and how far I still have to go. One of the times I look back on with mixed feelings was the year 2003. By this time I'd been reading professionally for clients for a few years, yet nothing could have prepared me for this period of my life. It was a hard time for me. Within a short span of six months, my beloved father died, I had to put my cherished horse down, and I was in a near-fatal car accident. Talk about catalysts for great shifts and growth!

While these events were personal tragedies at the time, they led me to discover greater spiritual strength within myself. This facilitated my being able to tune in to my psychic abilities on a much stronger level, amping them up even further. This period of spiritual self-discovery also led to a stronger connection to Divine spirit beings such as angels, spirit guides, and ascended masters. (Yes, they're available to all who seek them.) I wouldn't think of doing a reading, clearing of negative energy, or paranormal investigation without their aid, wisdom, and protection.

My strong connection with these powerful spirit beings is a main reason I no longer fear ghosts and the unknown. The other reason is that I now recognize ghosts for what they truly are: not scary things, but Divine spirits (albeit clueless ones) like you and me. Being able to work with them from this truth has allowed me to identify and interact with them from a place of love and compassion versus fear and scorn.

After all, before they were ghosts they were just as human as you, dear reader, and me.

I love what I do. Even more, I love using my God-given abilities to help others. I truly believe that everyone has these psychic abilities to some extent. Therefore, a main goal of this book is to educate people about the psychic process through positive exposure to the psychic world and its inhabitants. By doing this, it is my hope that readers will feel empowered by it, not threatened.

Happy journeying,
Boo

DENIZENS OF OLD DECATUR CEMETERY

Old Decatur Cemetery, haunted? You bet!

Located in Decatur, Georgia, this is one burial ground that effortlessly lives up to its otherworldly reputation. This city of the dead can go head to head with any of the other well-known haunted cemeteries in the country, such as those in New Orleans, Savannah, and Charleston.

When I say this, people typically respond, "Well yeah, Boo, it's a cemetery! What do you expect?"

"Not so," I answer. "Most cemeteries are relatively quiet when it comes to the paranormal. There aren't many ghosts."

There are two characteristics you want to check out when looking for a cemetery to investigate.

The first to consider is the human history of the area. Was there a great deal of human activity and historical events, such as a battle or other type of strife, that occurred on and around the cemetery grounds? Or none whatsoever? Your "area ghosts" are created from the living human sources who died with issues from these incidents. A lot of cemeteries haven't had much human strife and history occur around them. In other words, you need very upset human sources to create ghosts. (But rest assured, most spirits, when they leave the human body, move on to the Other Side—Heaven—with relative ease.)

The second characteristic to think about is what sources of energy are available for the ghosts to utilize. Ghosts can't manufacture their own energy. They no longer have a physical body with atoms, molecules, and biochemical processes for energy production. In the Ghost Realm, they've trapped themselves in an energy void. Their life force is low and weak. If they want to be active, they must take energy from other sources. They'll take it from anything inorganic (meaning nonliving), such as electronics, or organic (living sources), such as humans, plants, or animals.

Most cemeteries are now landscaped with artificial flowers at the grave sites and nothing else. The artificial flowers look nice and make cemetery maintenance easier, but if you're an energy-hungry ghost, you're not going to get your fix from them. Instead, you'll go to a cemetery where there's a surfeit of energy from living, natural landscaping, such as large trees and shrubs. Because they're living beings, these plants are able to manufacture energy, which the ghosts will then feed on. This gives them the energy to be more active, versus ghosts that trap themselves in more energetically sterile landscaping.

With this in mind, it's easy to see how old Decatur Cemetery lives up to its reputation as a paranormal investigator's delight. It's absolutely *loaded* with otherworldly types, as it fulfills both the needed characteristics for a paranormally active cemetery and then some!

First off, it's one of Georgia's oldest public cemeteries, having been created in 1826, three years after its namesake village, Decatur, was established. What unofficially adds years to its service as a burial ground, though, is that in the late 1700s there was an old church with its graveyard located on the grounds.

In its almost two centuries of existence, the old burial ground and its natural landscaping has witnessed its share of human drama and anguish. Is it any wonder that old Decatur Cemetery has acquired so many ghostly denizens over the years?

One of the most traumatic events that occurred in and around Decatur and its cemetery was the Battle of Atlanta, or the Battle of Decatur, fought during the American Civil War. Decatur was located six rural miles from Atlanta. Atlanta was one of the last major Confederate rail centers that had eluded Union capture. It was critical to the South for moving troops and supplies throughout the Confederacy. The Union command under General Ulysses S. Grant realized they had to capture Atlanta or the war would drag on.

General William T. Sherman was the Union commander put in charge of the Atlanta campaign. He came down from northwest Georgia at the head of a massive Union Army, ninety thousand strong. There was heavy fighting and skirmishing all the way to Atlanta. The Confederate resistance was desperate and fierce.

In the spring/summer of 1864, Sherman and his army finally reached the "gates" of Atlanta, yet he was unable to enter and capture the city at that time. General John B. Hood, the Confederate general in charge of the defense of Atlanta, had entrenched his troops all around the city.

In preparation for the coming battle on July 22, 1864, Sherman took over the Decatur area for use as part of the Union supply train. That set up Decatur as an unwilling area of the battlefield. On the day of the battle, the Union troops holding Decatur were taken by surprise and overrun by Confederate General Joseph Wheeler and his cavalry. When Wheeler's cavalry overran the Union lines, chaos erupted among the panicked Union soldiers.

The encounter turned into vicious, bloody, hand-to-hand combat.

The desperate fighting swirled around the old DeKalb County Courthouse, among the houses of the villagers, and throughout Decatur Cemetery. Many soldiers and army livestock were killed throughout the village and its cemetery that day before the Confederate cavalry drove the Union troops out of Decatur.

Yet the Confederates' victory was not to last. They couldn't hold the position because a shortage of Confederate troops necessitated Wheeler's cavalry being ordered to another area of the battle. This allowed the Union to reoccupy Decatur.

Sherman was unable to capture Atlanta itself on July 22. It was only after a brutal six-week siege that the city was forced to surrender on September 2, 1864. The eventual capture of Atlanta wasn't the only consequence of the bloody, desperate fighting that had taken place in and around Decatur and the other areas of battle.

What about some of the soldiers who were killed during the Atlanta campaign? Yep, they ended up trapped in the Ghost Realm, a common occurrence on battlefields everywhere. These ghost soldiers are some of the most issue-ridden spirits around. Some of the issues that can trap them in the Ghost Realm are extreme feelings of guilt, fear, grief, a sense of duty, and/or sadness. That's what happened to some of the thirteen thousand casualties that day.

When the dust cleared after the battle and the armies moved on to other battlefields, many of the dead continued fighting. Only now, their combat takes place in another realm: the Ghost Realm.

One of these ghost soldiers left behind in old Decatur Cemetery (among many others) is a Union cavalryman.

He and his horse are still there today, waiting to carry orders into battle that will never come. When the Confederate cavalry charged into the cemetery with guns firing and sabers slashing, they caught this soldier and his comrades by surprise. The hail of bullets instantly killed him and his horse, dropping them where they stood. His death was so sudden, he's still not aware that he and his horse are dead. When he was killed, he fell but then got up, not realizing that he had left his physical body behind in the dust. In fact, he probably gave a sigh of relief thinking he had escaped serious injury. When I see this ghostly duo, they're always standing at a corner formed by two cemetery roads. The cavalryman is ready to ride into battle at a moment's notice. He's gripping the left cheek strap of the bridle with his right hand as he holds the reins with his left in an attempt to control the horse. The horse, hearing the sounds of battle, is edgy and restless. He's snorting and stamping his hooves in anticipation, jostling the canteen against the saddle and jangling the bridle chains.

Visitors to the cemetery have told of hearing what sounds like a horse snorting and stamping around at this location, as well as hearing metal clanking and jangling.

This isn't the only location where ghost horses have been heard. People coming through the gate into the cemetery have heard a horse neighing and snorting behind them to the right. They quickly turn around but there's no horse there, at least not one they can see.

Neighbors of the old graveyard have heard the music of drums and bugles playing late at night in the dark cemetery that no one can explain. These battle drums and bugles must make the cavalryman feel right at home. Visitors have remarked about the large cold spot at the corner where the ghostly duo stand. It doesn't matter how hot the day is, this location is always cold. Needing energy, the two are continually taking the energy (heat) out of the air around them. Their ghostly presence is mute testament to a soldier so dedicated to his duty that he refuses to leave his post to move on. He and his mount faithfully wait, for no telling how long, to go into a battle that was already fought 150 years ago.

The cavalryman ghost is a nice guy, though, compared to another ghost I ran into in old Decatur Cemetery. People who walk and jog in the cemetery had told me about an area in the back, on the border, that they were not comfortable going through. The air on this stretch of the old road always had a feeling of menace and chilly creepiness to it. They always felt something watching them through hate-filled eyes. There was also the sound of footsteps that followed the women as they walked or jogged through this area.

Yes, there was definitely something or someone back there besides the occasional living person.

Some of the nineteenth-century graves in Old Decatur Cemetery

Being the curious type, I went searching for it. When I got there, the area was an island of doom and gloom compared to the lighter areas around it. And standing, or rather leaning against a tree, was the source of this heavy energy: a ghost. And not your run-of-the-mill ghost, either. He was about ten feet off the trail, hidden among some cedar trees. Every now and then he would glance down the trail as if waiting for someone. He was a short, brutish man bristling with deadly menace. His dark aura hinted at an earthly life that had been filled with violence and extreme cruelty.

I approached him with respect but no fear.

Ghosts are notorious for trying to scare or startle a person so they can take and utilize the human's energy for themselves. Humans can generate and renew their energy from their physical bodies, but ghosts can't. Spirits on the Other Side, even though they no longer have their physical bodies, have unlimited energy because they're in direct contact with the Source.

Most ghosts realize that when a human is frightened they'll go into a fight-or-flight response. This assures the human a burst of energy for use in a possible emergency. Ghosts take advantage of this human reaction to use the energy to recharge and strengthen themselves.

So, I certainly wasn't going to allow this guy to feel any more powerful than he already thought he was by feeding him my energy. The fact that I wasn't going to allow him to scare me nonplussed him. He'd been feeling mighty powerful from frightening everyone away. Then here came unprepossessing me, headed right for him! Taken by surprise, he glared hard at me as I walked up the hill toward him.

"Whadaya want?" he growled.

"I'm trying to find out who's haunting this area. Are you buried in this cemetery?"

"No!"

"Then what are you doing here?"

"None of your damn business!"

"What's your name?"

"Wouldn't you like to know, girlie!" he jeeringly shot back with an evil-looking leer.

This answer and the accompanying look confirmed my initial impression that he was an emotionally unstable, depraved individual. If he had given me this look while alive it would have made my skin crawl. This guy had truly not been burdened by any sense of right and wrong when in his physical body.

Despite his blatant antagonism, I addressed him calmly. I was curious to discover what was going on behind the sinister façade of this lost soul. In my years of working with ghosts of many different temperaments, I have rarely found one that couldn't be dealt with eventually. Look beneath the surface and there's a confused, lost spirit looking for help to find the peace that eluded them in life. This confused, fearful state is why, no matter how nasty the demeanor, I'm firm but also compassionate when working with ghosts. Staying in this nonjudgmental mode helps me to see the complete picture of the ghost's previous lifetime, and how it affected its decision to trap itself in the Ghost Realm.

But this was one ghost who was going to test my resolve to keep my energetic vibrations high. I would have to try not to censor him no matter what I heard.

As he glared at me, I clairvoyantly received pictures from his life. They weren't pretty pictures. He was telepathically sending them to me to gauge my reaction. Would my calm slip? Would I be startled, scared? By what I saw, I knew that if I'd run into this guy while he was alive I would have been absolutely terrified. Why? Because when alive, he'd been a serial killer preying on women! Yet as long as I didn't give him any energy, he couldn't harm me now, so I kept my cool. He didn't like that one bit.

Not getting the reaction he had hoped for, he crossed his arms and turned his back on me. I realized I wasn't going to get any more out of him, at least for the present. He wouldn't play the game unless we played by *his* rules. Like humans, ghosts can get on power trips and try to control everything. With a last "I'll see you later," I walked away, leaving him standing on his lonely hill.

A month later, I was working with a paranormal investigation team in Decatur Cemetery. They would be using their instruments to gather evidence while I channeled messages from the ghosts. I had already located three ghosts for the team to investigate. My acquaintance the serial killer was among the three.

It was just getting dark as we arrived at the cemetery. After finishing with the first ghost, I led them down to the back of the cemetery, bordered by woods. Even in the daytime it has a lonely, desolate feel. That night, the air around us felt heavy and dark. One of the team members couldn't help exclaiming, "Man, this is one creepy area! What's going on here?"

The presence of the ghostly serial killer was what was going on here. He stood just off the dirt path, glowering at us. The group set up their equipment while I approached the ghost to draw him into conversation. When I stopped in front of him, he turned his nasty attention fully on me.

"What's your name?" I asked.

"Lenny," he replied with a sly grin. I got the distinct impression he hadn't given me his real name, but it was a start. "I was never caught, you know!" he bragged.

Wanting to clarify what he was talking about, I asked, "What weren't you caught for?"

"What I did to all those women! I killed them, but first I had my fun. I was good at keeping them alive for a few days so I could play with them. You should have seen the tools I used. When I put my hands around their soft throats and strangled them, well, that was the best part. I loved to feel them gasping and struggling for their last breath as I held them down with my legs!" Even now as he relived his horrible actions, the ghost got excited, just as he had in life.

As he talked, I relayed his words to the group. Some parts of his narrative I withheld; they were just too graphic and disturbing. Lenny's victims ranged from a sixteen-year-old girl up to a twenty-eight-year-old woman. There had been many victims over the years.

At this point, members of the group jumped in and asked questions. They couldn't hear him, but he could hear them. I relayed the answers from the serial killer ghost.

"If you were never caught and executed for your crimes, then how did you die?" asked one.

"I got into a fight in a bar. The other guy had a friend who knifed me in the back, the bastard!" he answered hotly. How ironic that this guy, who had snuffed out others' lives with no remorse, was so angry and offended that someone had dared do it to him!

Someone else asked, "When were you active as a serial killer?"

"In the sixties. It was great! All those hippie chicks hanging out, looking for love. I gave it to them too!" he exclaimed with a hard laugh.

He started to expound once again on his gruesome activities, but I had had enough of his bragging. Wanting to draw his focus back to my questions, I was firm but nonconfrontational when I interrupted him. "If you're not buried here, what are you hanging out in old Decatur Cemetery for?"

He momentarily paused. I noticed that whenever he addressed me, his energy would soften slightly in response to my noncondemning tone. His softening energy reminded me of what my guides and angels had told me while preparing me to work with him. They had said, "Although he was unaware of this at the time he was committing his crimes, he was finishing out karmic business and soul contracts between him and his victims. This doesn't mean that his criminal activities are condoned and excused. There are always choices, and nothing is written in stone. But it's not your place to judge his soul either. You must keep your energy soft and nonjudgmental. Remember, appearances can be deceiving. Be firm, but if you judge him you will miss discovering who's really behind the serial killer façade."

In response to my calm energy, his voice lost some of its belligerent, adversarial quality. "The last woman I killed is buried here. I'm looking for her," he answered quietly.

Before I could ask why, another member of the group, who couldn't hear what Lenny and I were talking about, brusquely interrupted with, "Just what have you ever contributed to society?"

His tone was angry and confrontational, mirroring the group's feelings toward Lenny. Their disgust was understandable. His actions toward others had been heinous while alive. He truly was one upsetting individual.

Responding to the tone, Lenny turned away from us, refusing to answer the question.

The man aggressively threw the question at Lenny again. "What have you contributed to society, sicko?"

"Bodies!" Lenny venomously spat back. "Bodies!" The serial killer persona was back in full force. They couldn't hear what he was saying, just like they couldn't see him. But the nasty energy directed at the group was palpable.

"What did he say, what did he say?" they impatiently asked.

"Bodies! He said he contributed bodies to society," I finally told them.

That definitely got a reaction from the group. Lenny wore a look that was both smug and sneering. His mood had changed for the worse in response to the antagonistic energy of the group. The answer to my "why" would have to wait; there'd be no getting any more information from the truculent ghost tonight. It was time to leave. I wouldn't run into the serial killer ghost again until much later, when I was working with a group of ghost children in the cemetery.

***

For years, people visiting old Decatur Cemetery would mention hearing what sounded like children laughing and playing around them. Unable to see them, they dismissed the incidents as figments of their imagination. But whenever I walked through the cemetery, I would sometimes see these ghost children running and playing with each other. Over the years, the vast cemetery had become their playground.

These ghost children were a group of orphans buried in Decatur Cemetery in the aptly named Orphans' Section. There are twenty-five little headstones in this section, lined up in rows of five. The ghost children, when alive, had been wards of an orphanage established in 1871 in Decatur.

The orphans' plot at Old Decatur Cemetery

The Civil War created a lot of orphans throughout the country. So many men were killed in the war; the sheer number of whole families torn asunder was staggering. The man was the sole wage earner at this time in our country's history. A lot of women were left with four or more children to try to raise alone. To prevent the whole family from starving to death, some mothers were forced to make a horrible decision: which children to turn out of the family. Better some starve to death than all perish.

Also, because of the prevalence of different diseases of the times, it wasn't uncommon for both mother and father and some of the children to die from sickness, leaving the rest of the children true orphans. Sometimes church members would step forward to give the orphans a home. Often, though, the children would be placed in an orphanage. Orphanages came into being to pick up the slack for society.

During the Victorian era and into the first half of the twentieth century, most of the orphanages were nothing more than brutally cold institutions. Whether they were operated by a church, the state, or a private entity, the children didn't get much in the way of food and clothing. Emotional warmth and love were even rarer commodities. Many of the supervisors who managed the orphanages and their workers believed the children should be satisfied to have just the basics, such as food and shelter. Love? Why did they deserve that? Weren't they burdens on society? How dare they expect emotional warmth!

Society as a whole was having a rough time. The advent of the Industrial Revolution had ushered in great changes. A lot of those changes, such as child labor in the factories, were not for the better. For the lower classes and those in abject poverty, life was hard indeed. Death from malnutrition and fatal illnesses were common occurrences. Life was especially rough and uncertain for children. The records state that for children ten and under, the mortality rate was at least 60 percent in any given area, with the majority of these deaths occurring before the age of five.

The Decatur orphans were no exception. At the turn of the nineteenth century, twenty-five children at the orphanage died within a few years. Their passing was as unimportant and unnoticed as they themselves had been while alive. Nobody bothered to record their causes of death, or even mourn them. Many of the orphans' little headstones were left blank with no names or birth and death dates.

Death was their ticket out of their dreary existence, but it had not freed them from their main issue while alive: yearning to be loved. This issue now trapped them in the Ghost Realm. While alive, each little orphan had held on to the hope that there was someone out there beyond the orphanage who cared enough to come for them, to take them away. They would wake up each morning just knowing this could be the day it would happen. Each child had dreamed of a life with someone who would love and cherish them. Some had even been hopelessly waiting for their mother or father to come back to claim them. The desire to be special and loved had been so strong in these children, they took it with them to the grave. This yearning now held the group of Decatur orphans trapped in the Ghost Realm.

The comfort and security of the familiar had first brought the children together as a group. As each child had died and been buried, his or her spirit would seek out those who had preceded them in death. These were the companions they had known and been close to while living at the cold orphanage. The group of young spirits now stayed in the cemetery because, in their confusion, the only other place to go seemed to be back to the orphanage. They knew of no other place or people that would take them, but the dreadful orphanage hadn't wanted them either. That left old Decatur Cemetery.

The ghost children had no idea another place existed where they could find unconditional love and acceptance. This place, called Heaven or the Other Side, is a place of love and light, peace and joy. The children didn't know this, though. So here they had stayed for over a hundred years, roaming the cemetery and playing tag among the living who came to visit departed loved ones. Each little ghost was still waiting for someone to love them enough to take them away, freeing their spirit from the Ghost Realm.

After observing the ghost orphans from afar one day, I decided to try to help them. The afternoon had already faded into dusk when I arrived at the Orphans' Section. I found them running among the tombstones, joyfully laughing and calling to each other. As I stood on the dirt path beside their burial section, the ghost children paused in their play and started gravitating toward me. They were curious about the human who could see them.

The little ghosts gathered in a loose group all around me, shyness slowing their approach. I felt like Wendy standing among the children of Neverland. Finally, one young girl with shoulder-length hair stepped forward from the group. She was a slender, pale child of about ten or twelve years old. There was a careworn, weary energy about her.

"Hi, my name is Boo," I told her. "What's yours?"

"Janie," she shyly replied. She moved to stand in front of me. "Why are you here? How can you see us when other people can't?"

By now the other children had come closer to hear what we were saying. They ranged in age from as young as three or four years old up to Janie's age.

"Yeah, how can you see us?" piped up one little boy with dark, unruly hair and blue eyes.

"There are plenty of other people with abilities like mine, but most don't work with spirits like I do. It's all about being able to shift energetic frequencies to different levels," I answered.

That was the simplest way I could explain how psychic abilities work. It still wasn't simple enough, but it would have to do. Too much in-depth explanation and I might lose the children's attention, then off they would scatter to different parts of the cemetery. So, to forestall the questions I saw on the children's faces, I redirected their attention. "What was your life like in the orphanage?" I asked Janie.

"Rough." Despite the simplicity of the answer, I could still hear the emotional pain in the young ghost girl's voice. "The women who looked after us didn't care about us orphans at all. It was a job to them and nothing more. I tried to look after the young ones as best I could." Tears started slipping down her thin, pale cheeks. "One winter night, I heard one of the little girls crying on her cot. The dorm where we stayed was always cold and drafty. The little girl said she was cold and wanted another blanket. The lady said no, that she had what she was allowed. When the lady left, I got up to check on the little girl. She was shivering and crying from the cold. I gave her my one blanket. It did no good, though. They found her dead the next morning. She had died all alone and frightened. Sometimes my best wasn't good enough." Janie sobbed in deep despair. "I tried to look after my best friend, Viola, and her little brothers, Willie and John. I lost them too. One day I got sick. I was so tired, I just gave up and died. It didn't matter. I'd lost everybody in my life I loved. Nobody else would care if I lived or died. To the people in the orphanage, it meant one less mouth to feed."

"What happened to your parents, Janie?"

"Daddy caught the fever. There was no money for the doctor, so Mama nursed him. She caught it too, though, and they both died. Mama and Daddy's families couldn't handle the extra burden of more children, so they dropped us off at the orphanage."

By now Janie was crying uncontrollably from the memories of the sadness and despair she had lived with in her short life. I struggled not to cry myself after hearing her tragic life story. I knew I had to keep my emotions in check and balanced. If I didn't, it might break my connection with this group of ghost children. This disconnect can occur if my energetic vibrations become too low and heavy, such as from a heavy emotion like deep sadness. Then I won't be able to match ghosts' higher vibrations. To connect with ghosts and other spirits, you must be on the same energetic frequency. If not, it's like a radio station off the channel. The frequencies don't match and there's interfering static.

While I composed myself, the three-year-old boy holding Janie's hand pulled loose from her. He toddled over to me and wrapped his little, ghostly frame around my left leg. Intense cold from his small form spread through my entire body. He didn't have his own energy, so he was unintentionally taking all the energy (heat) out of my leg.

I normally wouldn't allow a ghost to initiate and maintain close contact with my physical body because of the drain on my energy. But this was a different situation. I didn't want to appear to reject the little boy like he had been rejected so many times in life. But I could feel my leg beginning to go numb from the intense cold. Eventually I wouldn't be able to stand on it. Janie, seeing my dilemma, tried calling the ghost child back to her. "Come on, Willie! Come stand by me like a good boy."

Yet her words only made him cling more desperately to my leg. He hadn't felt the security and comfort that comes from energetic contact with a warm human body in many years. She finally had to come over and pry him loose.

"It's okay, Willie. You can stay beside me," I reassured him.

He grinned up at me and I grinned back as I stroked his hair. Neither one of us could feel the gesture but we both understood the feelings behind it. We had become boon companions.

All of a sudden, one of the other ghost children pointed and whispered excitedly, "Miss Katty's coming! Miss Katty's coming!"

I looked and saw the pale ghost of a young woman gliding up the path toward us through the twilight. She was floating along about two feet above the ground. There were two or three children trailing along in her wake. The ghost glided up to me and stopped a foot away. As she floated in the air in front of me, I could feel the cold emanating off her ghostly form. She wore a plain, long, white dress that floated and swayed around her small, black, button-up shoes. Although she was plain of face, there was a kind air about her that made her quite attractive.

The ghost reached out and took my right hand in both of hers. "My name is Katherine," she said. "The children tell me your name is Miss Boo. I'm pleased to meet you."

"I'm pleased to meet you also, Katherine," I said, "but why are you still here in this cemetery? You're obviously aware you've died."

"These children are my charges," she replied. "I was one of the attendants in the orphanage when I was alive. I loved the children dearly and tried to make up for the lack of love and care from the other caretakers. When the children starting dying, there was nothing I could do. The orphanage was always so cold and damp. I felt so helpless. Then one cold winter, I contracted influenza from one of the children and died. At my funeral service, I was at peace. I was ready to cross over into the beautiful golden Light. Just when I was about to step in, a voice called out, 'Miss Katty, Miss Katty!' "

At my look of sudden puzzlement, Jamie interrupted, "Miss Katty is what the little children called Miss Katherine. They couldn't say her name right."

"It was me, it was me, Miss Katty!" a little redhaired girl chimed in.

"Yes, I know it was you, Elizabeth," Katherine assured the child with a loving smile. "When I turned around to see who was calling me, imagine my surprise and delight upon seeing my dear little ones from the orphanage. I knew what I had to do. I turned and walked away from the Light, choosing once again to look after my children. I won't cross without them, and some refuse to go."

"Why is that, Katherine?" I asked.

"They're worried that their mothers won't be able to find them if they leave. These are the young ones who've never given up hope of being reunited with their loved ones. The other children won't cross without them.

"So here we all are, trapped together in this empty, ghostly existence," she said with a sigh. Once again taking my hand in both of hers, she asked, "Could you help us, Miss Boo? Please, won't you help us if you can?"

There was such an air of weariness and desperation around Katherine when she said this that one couldn't help feeling a great sadness for the ghosts' plight. Neither she nor the children realized how much time had passed. They were all hanging around, waiting for their families to come claim them, families that had long since moved on. There was only one way, and one place, where they could be reunited with their loved ones: the Other Side.

"Katherine, are you aware of the Other Side—or Heaven, as some call it?" I asked her.

"Of course. From all I've heard, it's a most wondrous place!"

"Are you ready to cross over to the Other Side with the children if I can help you?"

"No, not yet. Three or four of the children are still out playing and I don't know when they'll come back," she explained.

Since I couldn't resolve the groups' dilemma now, it was time to go. It had already gotten late and dark in the cemetery. While I'm not scared of ghosts, I do get concerned sometimes with what two-legged, living individuals I might run into while by myself. Also, while the ghostly forms of the orphan group weren't tired from the lateness of the hour, my physical form was feeling it after being around so much otherworldly energy for an extended period.

I told Katherine that I would let her know ahead of time when I was coming back (by telepathy, the universal language—no phones here, by the way!). She assured me that she and Janie would do their best to have the children gathered together at that time. I parted company with the group of ghost orphans and their caretaker to a chorus of "Bye Miss Boo, bye Miss Boo!"

It was several months later before I could return to old Decatur Cemetery to help Miss Katherine and her charges. I sent the word ahead of time telepathically that I was on my way. True to her word, Katherine and Janie had all the children assembled at the Orphans' Section. I had brought along two friends, Lisalyn Jackson and Marta Irvington, to take photos. Also, when I'm channeling and working with spirits, I'm not totally in my physical body. I'm not as aware of the physical world around me. For safety's sake, Marta and Lisalyn would keep an eye on the physical world for me.

I walked through the group of ghost children into the Orphans' Section and sat on a low wall. Katherine stood off to my left supervising and gathering the children. Janie came over and sat close to me on my right side.

Trying to keep the quiver of trepidation out of her voice, Janie quietly asked me, "What's it like, Miss Boo?"

"I've never been all the way to the Other Side in this lifetime, Janie," I replied. "I can only go so far on that journey because my spirit is still inhabiting its physical body. It anchors my spirit in this earthly realm. The many spirits that I have communicated with, though, have all told me that it's the most beautiful place you can imagine. It's filled with angels and loved ones and is a realm of indescribable love, Light, peace, and great joy. All of your friends and family who have gone before you will be there. Even your beloved animal companions will be there to welcome you Home. If you wish for something, all you have to do is think of it and it's yours. There are no limitations on where you can go, what you can do, or who you can be on the Other Side. The angels are your playmates, if you wish. You're always protected and safe while there. No one can hurt you. It's truly paradise, Janie!"

Just then, the little boy, Willie, ran over to us. The little ghost pushed in and snuggled between Janie and me, pressing against my side. Looking up at me in delight, he gave me a delighted, snaggletoothed grin. "Hey, Miss Boo!"

As I looked down at him, I noticed the faint streaks cutting through the dirt on his face, caused by the tears he'd cried on the night he died. He'd felt frightened and alone, and the people caring for him hadn't offered much comfort, if any. Like all ghosts, when he'd trapped himself in the Ghost Realm he'd kept the physical countenance he died with. When spirits cross over to the Other Side, they go through a healing process. This healing erases marks such as wounds from murder, war, or emotional instabilities left over from any physical or emotional traumas.

As Willie told me about his adventures of the day, the energy around us began to lighten. This could mean only one thing: Divine beings were assembling all around us. Angels! The ghost children felt this energy shift also and excitement rippled through the group. I felt great joy knowing that the angels would soon be helping Janie,

Willie, and the other young ghost orphans heal from their previous tragic lives.

I grinned down at the little boy, asking, "Hey Willie, are you ready to go on a trip with the angels?"

He studied the brilliantly glowing beings all around us with lively interest. "Sure Miss Boo, it'll be fun!" he exclaimed with childish enthusiasm and trust.

Sudden movement beyond Katherine drew my attention. There, standing off a little way from her, was the ghost of the serial killer, Lenny! He was studying Katherine and the orphan children with intense interest.

Now what is he lurking about for?

In the next moment, though, I forgot all about the serial killer as the ghost children scrambled and ran to Katherine in answer to her call. She quieted the excited orphans, saying, "Children, children, please be quiet and listen. Miss Boo has something to say to us."

Looking around at all the eager, expectant young faces, I told them, "It's time for you children to leave the Ghost Realm where you've been trapped for so long. The angels are going to take you to the Other Side, where your families are waiting for you. Your families love you very much and can't wait to see you."

Trepidation flashed across the younger children's faces at the thought of leaving the familiar cemetery. I tried to reassure them. "There's nothing to be afraid of. The angels will watch over you and keep you safe. You're special and loved in their eyes."

An older boy interrupted me. "What if we have no one to come for us when we reach the Other Side? What will become of us then?" Other children were now nodding in agreement over this shared fear. I realized with some alarm that the children hadn't decided whether to cross or not. It would be their choice, after all. The look of anxiety on Katherine's face mirrored my concern.

"You have nothing to fear on the Other Side—or Heaven, as you've heard it called," I told them. "It's different than the Earth Realm, where you were abandoned when in the physical. On the Other Side, every spirit that crosses over has many other spirits that love them, so they'll never be alone. These angels will be your playmates and protective companions. You are so loved!"

As if in confirmation of this, the golden Light of the Divine portal opened in all its sparkling brilliance to my right. Awestruck, the children became very still. Then the stillness was broken by a little girl screaming excitedly, "Mama, Mama!" There, in the golden Light of the doorway, stood a young woman with her arms held out and tears streaming down her face. Then another woman appeared, and then an older man. "Papa, Papa!" cried out a little blond-haired boy. Angels were also there in the doorway, accompanying the spirits from the Other Side.

With no more doubts as to the outcome, Katherine joyfully said, "Line up, children, and form a line. We must maintain order."

I guess old habits can be hard to break sometimes. She was going to be their loving caretaker until the end! No longer sad, she was positively beaming with happiness and excitement, as were the children. After all these years, they were getting their greatest wish fulfilled. Loved ones had come to claim them and take them Home! With happy squeals of laughter and surrounded by their guardian angels, the group of ghost children skipped and ran into the Light.

Fittingly, Miss Katherine was the last to walk in. But before she disappeared into the portal, she turned and waved goodbye. "Thanks, Miss Boo." Then she was gone.

Before the golden portal closed around her, I saw the figure of a young man embrace her. As promised, there had been loved ones to greet each Homeward-bound spirit!

When the Light disappeared, I became aware once again of the dark, chilly cemetery around me. I also became aware of Lenny, the serial killer ghost, sitting on the side of a little dirt embankment, studying me. He beckoned me to him. I walked over and sat down next to him. He seemed much more subdued tonight than on our previous encounters. The attitude of callous, cynical bravado was gone and in its place was an air of uncertainty. For a few minutes we sat quietly side by side.

Finally I asked him, "What's up, Lenny?"

He got right to the point. "Do you think what happened to the children could happen for me?" he asked wistfully.

"Absolutely," I stated. "No one, no matter what they've done with their earthly life, is denied entrance to Heaven, the Other Side. All you have to do is ask in all sincerity and then decide to accept the Divine's grace. It's your choice and just that simple."

"Will you help me?" he hesitantly asked. He was afraid I might refuse him because of how he had lived his life while in the physical. Yet he was so desperate to find peace, he dared to ask anyway.

I answered, "Of course I'll help you, Lenny. It's not up to me to judge you. But first, please tell me why you have been looking for the spirit of your last victim who's buried in this cemetery."

"At first I didn't know why myself," he answered quietly. "After you asked me why when we first talked, I thought about it. I now know that I want to find her so I can ask her forgiveness for the terrible things I did to her. But I can't find her anywhere! Why can't I find her, Boo?" he asked in sudden desperation.

"Because, Lenny, her spirit is no longer here in this cemetery. She's crossed over to the Other Side. The only way to find her is to go there. Then you will find understanding and peace about why things happened the way they did in your physical life."

Just then, the Light appeared to our right. I could see the spirit of a young woman with long, brunette hair standing in it, beckoning to him. Pointing to the Light, I told him, "Look, Lenny, look over there! Who's that standing in the Light calling to you?" There was a moment of stunned silence from Lenny and then she called to him once again.

"Oh my God!" he gasped. "It's her!" Tears started streaming down Lenny's hard face. "What does she want with me, someone who hurt her so badly?"

"She wants you to accept her forgiveness," I explained to him.

"No, I can't. I can't even forgive myself!" he exclaimed in anguish.

"Yes you can, Lenny. That's why you need to go into the Light, cross over. On the Other Side you will find understanding and healing for yourself."

The young woman called again to Lenny.

"Go, Lenny. Everything will be all right." I reassured him. "This forgiveness is what you've really been searching for when you were looking for your last victim."

"Do you speak true, Boo?" he asked with dawning hope.

"Yes, Lenny, I speak the truth. I would never lie to a spirit," I answered in a serious tone. "Now go."

With that, he got up and hesitantly started walking toward the young woman and the Light. I could tell when he felt the joyful energy from the Other Side because he began to walk faster and faster toward it. When he reached it, the girl held out her hand with a smile and took his.

With an answering smile, he stepped through the portal and into the Light. The Light grew smaller and smaller and then was gone.

Once again, I was left alone in the dark cemetery. But the place Lenny was going would be filled with Light and perfect love. He'd be all right.

I'd be all right also, for I wasn't alone after all. Marta and Lisalyn were still sitting on the wall, quietly talking. They had patiently waited for me to finish my work with Lenny. Who but true friends would go with you into a dark, deserted cemetery at night to work with ghosts? I am truly blessed!

I MUST STAND FIRM

Have you ever had a cannonball fired into your head? Of course not, or you wouldn't be here to answer... right? Or would you? Well, some have had that happen, and yes, they're here to tell us about it. I'm talking about battlefield ghosts!

Okay, maybe the ghost wouldn't *tell* you so much as *show* you. Then there's no way you could miss the ghost's cause of death, what with him standing in front of you with half his head blown away! Now, as if this visual wasn't enough to make you feel faint, what about the fact that the ghost isn't aware he's missing part of his head? In other words, he's unaware of his gruesome demise. To him, he's still in possession of his head and there's a battle to be fought!

This ghost soldier was one of many I encountered the afternoon I visited Chickamauga Battlefield. Chickamauga Battlefield is located in what is now called the Chickamauga and Chattanooga National Military Park located on the Georgia-Tennessee border. It's one of the oldest military parks in the United States, having been dedicated on September 19, 1895. The park commemorates the series of battles that were fought between the Union and Confederate forces while trying to gain control of Chattanooga, Tennessee. Chattanooga was an important rail center essential to the

Southern war effort. It was considered the gateway to the Deep South and the important Confederate rail center of Atlanta, Georgia.

The first and largest battle of this effort was the Battle of Chickamauga, fought on September 19–20, 1863. Before the battle was waged on that beautiful fall morning, neither side's soldiers realized that they were about to be participants in the second most bloody battle of the War between the States.

The battlefield was a scene of massive carnage and death. The destruction was widely spread along battle lines that extended three and four miles in length. These battle lines ranged and shifted around deep Chickamauga Creek and its surrounding areas. The terrain in these areas was thickly wooded, swampy, and hilly—terrain not suited for efficient, effective fighting by 1800s standards.

Because of the rough terrain and heavy woods, communication between officers and their men on both sides was terrible or nonexistent. Soldiers became separated and lost from their comrades in the dense forest. Chaos and bloody carnage was the order of the day.

The Cherokee, the earlier inhabitants of the area, had named the creek Chickamauga. On September 19 and 20, it lived up to its name, which translates to "river of death." Witnesses said the creek ran red with blood. The two days of fighting claimed between thirty-four thousand and thirty-five thousand casualties. This total equaled about one third of all troops who fought in the battle.

After the two days of fighting, the Confederates emerged victorious, but their celebration was not to last. General Braxton Bragg, the incompetent commander of the Confederate forces, failed to take advantage of this costly victory when he dithered and delayed pursuing General William

Rosecrans and his Union army. This allowed Rosecrans and his forces to escape back to Chattanooga. The South had lost the opportunity to recapture Chattanooga, thus opening up the gateway to the Deep South to Union advancement.

The Union victory at the Battle of Chattanooga in November 1863 under Ulysses S. Grant put the Union in firm control of the area. The Deep South and its war industries were now wide open. It was at this point that Grant turned General William T. Sherman loose on Atlanta and the Deep South. Atlanta would be captured one year later, with the end of the war following shortly after.

But what about the dead, both Confederate and Union, who were left behind at Chickamauga when the armies moved on? What happened to them? A few hours after the battle, witnesses reported seeing women with lanterns walking around the dark battlefield calling and looking for wounded and dead loved ones and trying to minister to the other wounded. It was an eerie scene! Witnesses described how the screams and cries for help from the many wounded men could be heard throughout the night.

As the long night wore on, the screams and cries from the dark battlefield became weaker and weaker. Before the morning came, many of the wounded had died agonizing deaths. It's no wonder that Chickamauga can lay claim to being one of the most haunted battlefields anywhere! Tourists and staff tell of still hearing the phantom screams of the dying from that long-ago battle.

And what happened to the bodies of these thousands of dead soldiers? If you were Confederate, your body was buried soon after the battle. But if you were Union? Well, your corpse was given the same treatment the Confederate dead were given after the Battle of Gettysburg. The corpses lay for weeks where they fell in battle, desecrated by scavengers, both human and animal, and the weather. Eventually, the majority of the Union dead were buried in unmarked graves right where they died. Others were buried in trenches in mass graves—at least, what was left of the bodies was buried.

This careless, haphazard burying resulted in bodies being interred under the ground all over Chickamauga Battlefield. It's literally a vast, planted field of human remains. Even today, park maintenance staff doing work on the battlefield will unexpectedly dig up the earthly remains of dead soldiers from long ago.

But what about the *unearthly* remains of these thousands of dead soldiers? Did their spirits move on to the Other Side, or are many still here in ghost form? And if so, what would cause these thousands of ghosts to continue cluelessly fighting a battle that was already waged? Oh sure, some ghost soldiers do have personal reasons like anger, regret, etc., for refusing to move on to the Other Side, but for most ghost soldiers, what is the common denominator, the reason, for their self-entrapment in the Ghost Realm?

It was this question that drew me to the Chickamauga and Chattanooga National Military Park. I wanted to get the answer from the "horse's mouth" (please pardon the cliché), the ghosts themselves, as to why many soldiers get trapped on battlefields in the Ghost Realm after they're killed. When killed, the majority of soldiers move on to the Other Side where Divine Peace awaits. Yet, there are enough left behind to make battlefields some of the most haunted locations in the world. As it happens, Chickamauga is one of the premier haunted battlefield locations to be found anywhere! Not only did it play host to one of the bloodiest battles of the War between the States, the Civil War, but it's also served throughout the years as a place to dump the bodies of local murder victims. Even murder victims from farther away have been deposited there. Chickamauga Battlefield's thick, secluded woods and the lingering, heavy energy of the many battlefield dead also seem to draw suicides. Bodies have been found hanging from trees, or leaning against rocks, dead from a self-inflicted bullet wound.

And let's not forget the many troops who died there while going through basic training to fight in the Spanish-American War in 1898. Conditions were crowded, unsanitary, and mismanaged at Camp Thomas, as the Chickamauga training grounds were called. Typhoid fever broke out and ran rampant among the troops. Because of this, more troops succumbed and died from the fever than were killed in the Spanish-American War.

More ghosts added to old Chickamauga!

Well, by now you can probably deduce from the narrative that I love not only ghosts, but history! Since Chickamauga has both in spades, it was only logical for me to want to visit the old battlefield. I not only wanted to find out the whys and hows of its history, but also to meet some of its ghosts.

I couldn't wait!

Maybe that's why, instead of waiting for warmer weather like a less impulsive person would've done, I started my haunted-battlefield adventure at the tail end of a freezing-cold, windy fall day. The sky was gray and overcast that afternoon, as was the battlefield itself. The dark of night would be upon us in a couple of hours. I wasn't too concerned, though, as much of the vast battlefield is open twenty-four hours a day because of the many public roads that run through it.

On the other hand, one of my best friends and kindred spirits, Beth, was rather concerned about getting caught in the ever-darkening woods, especially after the man we stopped to talk to at the park entrance told us, "It's a beautiful place when the sun is out, but you don't want to get caught in the woods after dark. Unexplained things happen in them." I couldn't decide if he was serious or not, but Beth's suddenly still demeanor showed she was taking his admonishment seriously. To help her gain enthusiasm for our ghostly adventure (after all, who else did I have to take photos if she bolted?), I asked him if he was kidding. "No ma'am, I've lived here all my life. Strange things happen on that battlefield at night."

I didn't ask what strange things occurred, but that didn't stop the loquacious, older man from continuing anyway.

"People hear screams, men's voices, cannons firing, horses galloping, and then there's the lights that are seen bobbing through the woods. None of it can be explained. Oh, and then there's Ol' Green Eyes!"

Okay, my well-known curiosity got the better of me. I couldn't resist asking, "Who's Ol' Green Eyes?"

"Nobody knows who or what he is, but plenty of people have seen him through the years. My own cousin saw him late one night when he was driving through the battlefield coming from work. Some of the rangers have also seen him over the years, but I hear they're now supposed to keep quiet about such things."

"What does this Green Eyes look like?"

"My cousin said it had two bright-green, glaring eyes and stringy, long hair. It was big, like a big animal, but it was walking on two legs. It had big jaws with large fangs coming out of its mouth. He said it scared him so much when it jumped out in front of his car, he almost wrecked."

By this time Beth was starting to look uncomfortable. Ghosts were one thing, but whatever this was, was something else. So, not wanting Beth to be spooked any more than she already was, I quickly thanked the man and told him goodbye.

Seeing Beth's now-troubled face, I thought, *Well, that's that. He's leaving just in time.*

But no, before our newfound fount of information disappeared around a curve in the trail, he turned back and hollered, "Oh, they found the body of a murdered man in the woods last year! Y'all be careful!"

Just great! I thought, but maybe Beth hadn't heard.

It was obvious she had heard, though, when she said, "Okay Boo, everybody knows how you get when you're working with ghosts. You lose track of time. Promise we'll be out of the battlefield woods before dark."

It's true. When I'm working in the Ghost Realm, I'm energetically in a realm that doesn't have linear time like the Earth Realm does. In fact, there's no time. This is why, besides the usual influence of the typical ghostly confusion, a lot of ghosts don't realize how much time has passed between their death and the present.

Realizing that time was short to both keep my promise and work with the ghost soldiers, I quickly acquiesced. I may be an adventurous, impetuous woman, but I'm still a woman of my word—to both human and ghost. So, we hurried to one of the main areas of the battlefield called Snodgrass Hill.

Civil War monument at Snodgrass Hill, Chickamauga Battlefield, Chattanooga National Military Park

A man had already told me about his family's experiences at this location. He said it had felt creepy and that his family had felt something watching them the whole time. "It's funny, but I didn't hear or see any birds either," he had said.

His wife had felt so spooked (no pun intended!), she had told him, "Something's not right here. I want to leave!" For once, they were in total agreement about something.

In fact, many visitors have mentioned feeling strange and uneasy at this battlefield location. Little did they know how correct they were about the energy they picked up, created by what happened here over a hundred years ago. Snodgrass Hill was where the Union troops under General George H. Thomas made a determined, successful stand to stop the Confederates from overrunning the retreating Union army. The Hill's terrain was one of the roughest, most treacherous combat areas of the whole battlefield. This worked in favor for the outnumbered Union troops who were entrenched on top of it. The Confederate soldiers had to struggle up through the rough, uneven terrain under heavy Union fire. Wave after wave of these soldiers were ordered to charge, but all they succeeded in doing was add to the growing piles of corpses lying on Snodgrass Hill. Then it became a matter of not only trying to crawl and run over the rough landscape, but also over the bodies of dead comrades.

So yes, it's understandable how this location could have such a heavy, oppressive feel to it. But aside from this gloomy energy created from the hundreds of violent, horrible deaths that occurred here, what about the desperate, terrified energy emanating from the dead soldiers themselves—their ghosts?

And let's not forget Ol' Green Eyes, the terrifying "something" you'd hate to encounter in the thick, dark woods. He has been seen numerous times on and around Snodgrass Hill. So what, or rather who, is watching visitors as they explore the Hill?

Since I like to be in the thick of things, paranormal and otherwise, Snodgrass Hill promised to allow me to be just that. I couldn't wait!

When we arrived that late afternoon, there was no one else around. Freezing weather and smart people, remember? The place was deserted. We had the location to ourselves . . . or did we? I was about to find out!

As we left the parking lot behind and walked up Snodgrass Hill, we became aware of a deep, heavy, chilling energy permeating the area. This oppressive energy couldn't be solely attributed to the gloomy, overcast day. As we drew closer and closer to the woods with their gray stone monuments, the temperature kept dropping, getting colder and colder. The monuments were spread throughout the deep woods. Everywhere you looked, they were there, bearing weathered witness to the heavy fighting and dying that had occurred many years ago. Each of these stone monuments marked the different Confederate troop positions by home state.

We were still in the cleared-off area of Snodgrass Hill when Beth decided she'd like to stay in it rather than enter the brooding woods. So, up the Hill she took herself to where the Union positions had been. I, left to my own devices and agenda, headed for the dark, chilly woods. The closer I drew to them, the more I became aware of whispery overtones and shadowy movements among its trees. No, not the movement of birds and animals, for I had neither seen nor heard any wildlife in the woods.

As I entered those woods, I knew I was in the right area, for the sense of foreboding increased. As I continued down the trail I became aware that I was being watched. But that was okay, for I was watching them back! Yes, I was now walking among the ghosts of the Confederate dead, and there were so many! They were all over the woods. Some knew I was there, others didn't. The ones that didn't were so deeply trapped in the Ghost Realm that to them, no other realm or dimension existed. Because of this, they were more prone to walk or run through my body as they hurried to their ghostly battle positions. I wasn't there, at least to them, so there was no reason to avoid colliding with me.

The other ghost soldiers who were aware of me were at least cognizant to some degree of the other realms around them, one being the realm of the physically alive. But even they were still so confused, they didn't possess a true grasp at any given time as to what was real and what wasn't. Hence the long-ago battle they were still fighting and striving to win in the Ghost Realm. Whether they were aware or not as to their true state of existence, the sheer number of trapped ghost soldiers on Snodgrass Hill indicated a shared, unresolved issue. What was it, and did the ghosts themselves realize what it was?

Determined to find out, and see if I could maybe help some of them, I sat down on the stone monument denoting the battle position of the Third Regiment South Carolina Infantry. Sitting there looking around, I knew I wouldn't have long to wait before the dead noticed me. Or at least I hoped I didn't have long, for the late-afternoon light was starting to wane and early twilight was fast approaching.

Monument marking South Carolina brigade's battle position on Snodgrass Hill

As I sat on the cold, stone monument marker, shivering in the increasing gloom and chill of the woods, I noticed a grayish mist spreading over the area. Wherever the mist went, a deep cold followed. As it rolled around my body, the chill was so intense, I clutched my coat even tighter around me. I could see more Confederate ghost soldiers materializing out of it and around me, moving into battle positions.

All was still now except for the ghost soldiers slipping through the woods to step into their places of death. As I continued to watch the ghosts, I became aware that one soldier had paused and was now watching me. Deciding that I was safe to approach despite my strange clothing, he hurried over to me. He couldn't have been more than seventeen years old, maybe even younger. He had shaggy, shoulder-length, dark-brown hair and there was concern in his earnest, hazel eyes.

"Ma'am, this is a dangerous place for you! What are you doing here? Are you lost?"

"No, I'm not lost. My name is Boo and this is no longer a dangerous place."

"Yes it is, ma'am!" he said. "There's a fight fixin' ta happen. We're gonna take this hill from the Yanks!"

Thinking to tell him, "Oh no you're not," but knowing that would be addressed later, I instead asked him his name.

"Thomas Mason, ma'am."

Other Confederate ghost soldiers, comrades of his, paused in their battle preparations to observe us.

"Where are you from, Thomas?"

He gestured at his fellow soldiers. "Me and the boys are from South Carolina. My daddy was a preacher in Columbia. He's a man who always preached peace. He told me that sometimes there's a time to fight though, and this is it. So I joined up. Mama hated to see me go. She and my little sister cried and cried, but they knew it was right. I had to defend the homeland. I hope to make them proud!"

Looking at the bloody, gaping wounds in Thomas's chest and stomach that had splattered blood and entrails all over the front of his uniform, I thought, *You did, Thomas, you did . . . but at what cost? And you never made it home to bask in their pride . . .*

Pointing to a soldier who had walked up on his right, Thomas informed me, "This here's Henry. He's from my hometown. We grew up together. Now we're fighting together."

Also dying together, I thought with even deeper sadness.

Henry gave me a shy grin, not realizing that the smile on the right side of his mouth and cheek didn't match the left side, mainly because the right side wasn't there anymore. It had been blown away by a large-caliber bullet.

As Thomas and I continued talking, seven or eight other Confederate ghost soldiers materialized in front of and around me. All of them had terrible mortal wounds from the battle they had been killed in. One young man whose hair would have been a beautiful sandy-blond color now had brownish-red hair, colored like rust from the blood that had flowed when a shell of some kind blew away part of the left side of his face and head. Another ghost soldier, well, I had no idea what he had looked like because his head was no longer there.

Was Thomas aware of his horrible wounds? Not at all, as were none of the other ghost soldiers. They stood there soberly observing me. Then one young ghost soldier in the back of the group broke the reserve of his comrades when he pointed the shredded remnants of his shattered right arm at me and hollered, "Hey ma'am, where's your rifle? You look like a feisty one and we could sure use you!"

The group of ghost soldiers broke into raucous laughter at the vision of a scrawny woman, me, clawing her way up the steep hill to take it from the enemy.

"Yes ma'am, you could sure show these boys how to fight!" another ghost drolly stated to the accompaniment of more good-natured laughter.

Now I admit that I'm a feisty woman at times when I believe in a cause, but this wasn't my battle, nor was it theirs any longer. But how to convince them of this? Before I could find a way, Thomas unwittingly provided one for me when he turned serious once again. "All kidding aside, ma'am, why are you here? A woman and a civilian at that! There's hard, brutal fighting ahead!"

At his words, you could feel the ghost soldiers' moods swing back to somberness. Their previously raucous, carefree behavior had been nothing more than a façade, one meant to mask the true emotion that lurked underneath this thin veneer: great, almost overwhelming fear of the coming battle. Oh sure, when alive and faced with the real upcoming battle, they'd done their best to control it, to numb this fear. But each one had wondered if they'd be the first to break and run from the sheer brutality and horror when the time came to face it. They'd already experienced the horrors of previous battles, so they had no illusions as to what awaited them. Yet each soldier had known that he must stand firm once again for his brothers-in-arms. I could hear these thoughts playing over and over in the ghost soldiers' minds, long after the real fight on Snodgrass Hill had ended. "I'm afraid, but I must stand firm! I'm afraid, but I must stand firm!"

That was it! Duty to their comrades for whom they must stand firm was the common denominator, the main, shared issue that trapped many soldiers in the Ghost Realm on the battlefields where they had died. This was the great, ingrained issue they had carried with them not only into battle, but also into death.

It was easy to see how a soldier killed in battle could, in a confused mental and emotional state, step out of his ruined physical body and keep running across a battlefield year after year after year as a clueless ghost soldier. He had to face his fear and finish the fight, because he couldn't let his friends and comrades down. The only problem was, now with his death, he was unable to finish it. He was now trying to fight the battle in a different realm, a different dimension, than the one he had started out fighting in, the physical realm.

Did these Confederate ghost soldiers even know they were dead? I needed to find this out if I was going to possibly help them move on to the Other Side where Divine Peace awaited. I turned to Thomas to ask him about his death, but the impatient ghost soldier once again took the initiative.

"Ma'am, we don't have much time. Why are you here?"

Okay, here goes, I thought as the other ghost soldiers leaned in closer to hear how this peculiar female, me (it's not enough that a lot of the living think I'm peculiar, the ghosts think I am also!), was going to answer the question.

Knowing my answer was going to be unpopular and shocking to the assembled Confederate ghost soldiers, I took a steadying breath and let fly. "I'm from the present time in American history where the Confederacy is no more."

One of the ghosts quickly exclaimed, "What's this you're talking about, no more?"

"The war is over," I answered. "The South lost."

"Whadya mean, the South lost?" asked a dark-haired young soldier with beautiful blue eyes (at least, they would've been beautiful if one hadn't been shot out when he took a bullet to the forehead).

"Don't you know you're dead?" I asked the group.

"We're not dead! We're still waiting to get into the fight. Our officers say we've got to take this ridge from the Bluebellies, and we'll do it, by God!" another young ghost soldier stated with the conviction and enthusiasm of youth.

Despite this bravado, the fear running through the group was palpable. It was now obvious that none of these ghost soldiers were aware that they and their comrades had lost their physical bodies. They didn't see each other's mortal wounds like I did. To them, they were physically hale and hearty and ready for a fight, as were the other ghost soldiers now slipping quietly through the woods all around us, moving into position for the fight.

Noticing them, Thomas once again urgently told me, "Ma'am, we've got to go! The assault is starting. Try to find cover so you're not caught in the crossfire!"

How touching, I thought. *This young man, about to go into a brutal battle, is still concerned for another.*

But his first duty was to his comrades. That's why, when his ghostly comrades turned away to take their places in the advancing ghostly Confederate line, he started to hurry after them. I was on the verge of losing the opportunity to help these ghost soldiers. In desperation, I almost screamed it: "Wait, Thomas!"

He and his comrades turned back to me in alarm. Pausing, they waited for Thomas as he hurried back to me, exclaiming, "What is it, ma'am?"

Knowing there was no time to attempt to soften the blow, I bluntly asked him, "You do know you're dead, don't you?"

He stared at me as if I had gone crazy. Meanwhile, the woods on the slope above and around me had come alive with ghost soldiers. They materialized out of the icy mist that now surrounded us and permeated the woods in the approaching twilight. The otherworldly energy was building up to the ghostly battle once again—an otherworldly battle Thomas and his dead comrades seemed doomed to fight forever.

Cannon ready to repel the Confederate charge up Snodgrass Hill

Again I asked the now-stunned Thomas, "Do you not realize that you and your comrades are dead? Look around you. Can you not see that you, your comrades, and the other soldiers have no physical bodies to fight with? They were destroyed by your deaths in the fighting over one hundred and fifty years ago!"

At my words, I could see a growing mutinous look of denial spreading across Thomas's face. His next words confirmed this when he adamantly exclaimed, "I don't believe you, ma'am! There's something not right about you!"

Well now, there were times when more "normal" individuals might agree with the ghost, but now wasn't one of them. For one thing, I was the spirit still inhabiting its genuine, physical body, not he, no matter how hard he wanted to believe otherwise. But how to get through the strong resistance he had to accepting the truth of his death? I knew I was almost out of time when the ghost soldier turned and walked away, saying, "I'm sorry for your indisposed condition, ma'am, but I must leave you to join my comrades. They're depending on me, and if I don't go I'll be branded a coward. I must go! I bid you farewell and Godspeed."

I now knew the main issue that was trapping Thomas and his fellow soldiers in the Ghost Realm: the great fear that in the brutality and heat of battle they would be the one to turn coward and run. This cowardice would cause the soldier to be derelict in his duty to stand firm for his comrades, to finish the fight.

Had I learned this too late? I had yet to convince Thomas he was no longer of the physical realm, much less convince him to cross over to the Other Side where peace waited. Even now, he had almost caught up with his impatient comrades. I only had time for one last, desperate attempt to reach him through his confusion.

"Thomas!" I called to his retreating back. "Please shake my hand. I want to shake the hand of a brave man!"

He turned and walked back. With a lopsided grin, he held out a grimy, bloody hand and said, "All right, ma'am. Wish me luck!"

I put my own out for him to shake. Much to his stunned horror, his pale hand passed right through mine. He tried again and once more he was unable to grip my flesh-and-blood hand with his ethereal one.

"What is this?" he asked in great alarm.

At Thomas's cry of distress, his comrades rushed back to his side. "Thomas, what is it man, what's wrong?" one of them hollered.

"This lady claims that we're dead . . . that we're—we're ghosts!" Thomas stuttered back in alarmed confusion.

"Nonsense," another ghost soldier stated adamantly. "She's crazy!"

Okay, I'd about had enough of being called crazy for one day! Looking Thomas straight in the eye, I firmly told him, "Thomas, tell your comrades what happened when you tried to shake my hand."

He hesitated for a moment, still shaken and trying to make sense of what had happened. Then, haltingly, he told them how he had been unable to grip my hand with his. When he finished, another ghost soldier, a boy of about sixteen years with horrific leg and hip wounds, limped forward to place his hand on my shoulder. As with Thomas, his ghostly hand passed right through me. I felt no pressure. The only thing I did feel was the deep chill left by the ghost's hand as it went through my body, taking my energy. He jumped back in alarm, looking at his hand in horror.

"Why is this? Why can't I touch you?" he asked in a tone of growing dread.

"Because you, like your comrades here, don't have physical bodies anymore," I answered. "You're all dead. Your physical bodies were killed in the battle. Many years have passed since then. The only thing that remains of you is your eternal spirit."

"This can't be true! This can't be true!" he whispered to himself over and over.

Then he started sobbing as the realization hit that for him, there would be no more tomorrows. He would never again see his childhood sweetheart. He had left her waiting for him to come home in glory so they could begin their life together. Thomas and the other ghost soldiers crowded around their distraught young comrade, trying to comfort him.

Finally, Thomas turned back to me. "What about the battle? What of our comrades? Did they win the day?"

I quietly answered, "The battle is long since over. The Confederates won the battle but lost the war. As a result, the two sides, the North and the South, were once again united into one strong whole. But the physical realm, the Earth Realm, is not your concern anymore, Thomas. You and your fellow ghost soldiers are no longer a part of it."

"But we didn't finish the fight! We let our comrades down!" he stated sorrowfully.

"You fought the good fight while alive," I reassured him. "You gave it your best, your life. You can do no more than that. Your fight is done. You didn't let your comrades, family, or cause down. Don't you think it's time for you to give up the fight and find peace?"

"But what now? What is to become of us?" another ghost soldier anxiously interrupted.

"Why, if you choose to, you'll return to your true Home on the Other Side. The place Thomas's father and others preached about called Heaven. Heaven, or Nirvana as it's sometimes called, is the original, real Home spirits return to when they're finished with their physical life in the Earth Realm."

The mention of Thomas's father brought a knowing grin to his face. "Daddy sure did speak highly of the place, he did! Loudly too!" His fond words about his father let me know that his and the other ghosts' energies were starting to lighten up.

"But how do we get there?" asked the sixteen-year-old.

Before I could answer him, he stepped back, startled, as he suddenly spotted the angels beginning to assemble. The other ghost soldiers were now also staring in wonder at the shining beings all around us. Their loving, compassionate energy was infectious. I watched in growing wonder myself as the battle-hardened ghost soldiers' faces relaxed into joyful smiles of peace.

One of the ghost soldiers gasped, staring at a big, dark-haired angel. Pointing at the smiling angel, he exclaimed,

"Why, I saw you on the battlefield that day! You were holding one of the dead Alabama boys in your arms. In the next instant, you were gone. I thought it was my imagination playing tricks on me in the heat of battle and the heavy gun smoke."

The angel's smile grew broader as I explained to the astonished ghost soldier, "No, what you saw wasn't caused by your imagination that day. It was real. The angel was there to comfort the dying soldier. He was getting ready to escort the soldier's spirit, once it moved out of its ruined physical body, back to its true Home, the Other Side, if he chose to go. For you see, even on an active battlefield, no one ever dies alone and unloved. The angels are always there, lovingly ready to help the spirits find their way back Home when their transition time comes."

"What about my girl, will she be there?" the sixteen-year-old excitedly asked.

"What about my family?" Thomas asked with sudden hope.

Their comrades quickly joined in, their questions tumbling over themselves. Answering them honestly, I said I didn't know, but if they crossed over to go Home, they would find out for themselves. It was the only way to get their questions answered.

"Yes, but how do we do this?" another ghost asked.

As if in answer to his question, the golden Light materialized in front of the group. The Confederate ghosts stared at it in wonder and awe, their faces lit up by the golden sparkle emanating from the Light. Smiles of joy broke out on their rough, gunpowder-stained faces as they recognized the Light for what it was: the doorway to the tunnel that leads to the Other Side, Home.

At long last, they were now ready to return Home, a Home where there would be no opposing sides to fight for and causes to die over. As if to strengthen their resolve to cross over, loved ones appeared in the doorway.

"Mary Ann!" the sixteen-year-old hollered as he ran toward the Light.

The other Confederate ghost soldiers were more restrained in their excitement, still holding to their duty to stand firm for their comrades. They would leave no ghost soldier from the regiment behind. They would finish the fight together. And who should be bringing up the end of the line of marching ghost soldiers but Thomas himself? True to his character to look after others, he would be the last soldier to enter the Light. But before he did, he turned back and, giving me a happy, boyish grin, snapped a salute at me. Then he was gone.

My battlefield adventure was done and it was time for me to go also. Just in time, for here came Beth, flashlight in hand, to remind me about getting out of the woods by nighttime. The thing is, even though the dark of night was now approaching, the woods didn't seem so dark anymore.

So, the next time you stroll across a battlefield thinking how peaceful it looks, pause for a moment and tune in to what (or who) might be around you. You might be shocked to realize that you're right in the thick of a raging battle, even if it's an otherworldly one!

I'M STILL THE MASTER OF REDCLIFFE PLANTATION

It was a dark and stormy night when my good friend Christen Blass and I drove up the long, winding drive to the deserted antebellum mansion called Redcliffe. The force of the storm was whipping the tree branches wildly around, making them appear as ghostly arms reaching out for us.

Okay, okay, enough of the Gothic drama! I just always wanted to say that! In reality, it was a beautiful, early spring day and there wasn't a cloud in the blue sky when we drove up the long driveway to the Redcliffe Plantation mansion. And no, it's not deserted either. It's true that no one lives in the mansion now, at least nobody (or would that be no body) living. But you can hardly call it deserted, for the mansion and its grounds comprise Redcliffe Plantation State Historic Site. Besides the state park ranger on duty during the day, there's a caretaker always on the premises for security purposes. The mansion is located near the banks of the Savannah River, a few miles from the tiny town of Beach Island, South Carolina.

The master's house, Redcliffe Mansion

The ranger on duty the day we visited Redcliffe was Liza Simpson. She was the one who would give us our tour of the mansion and its grounds. Liza turned out to be a knowledgeable, personable individual. When we asked her about the possibility that the old mansion had ghosts, she told us that despite having never witnessed anything paranormal herself, she tried to keep an open mind to the possibility that Redcliffe was haunted.

"I can't do otherwise," she stated, "because there have been too many reports over the years from fellow staff members and visitors of strange, unexplained activity in and around the old mansion."

She told us that one such ghostly sighting reported over the years was the apparition of a young woman. Stunned visitors have watched as this ghostly lady descends the grand staircase in the main hall, dressed in a fashionable, long gown from the turn of the nineteenth century. The encounter might last only a moment before the ghost disappears.

"No matter," Liza said, "she has made an indelible impression on our visitors."

Liza's statement that the ghost often suddenly disappears brought up the point that to the observer, as in most human-ghost encounters, the apparition just seems to vanish, leaving the scared human witness feeling relieved. I always find this relief amusing (after all, I'm known for having a mischievous sense of humor!), for the human's relief would be short lived if they realized what had really happened. In most cases, the ghost has gone nowhere! All that changes is the energetic frequencies between the living person and the ghost.

When a person gets frightened or startled, their energetic vibrations are lowered. As a result, their energetic frequencies and those of the ghost are no longer on the same wavelength, hence the lost visual reception by the human. The "vanished" ghost could meanwhile still be standing there observing the now clueless, relieved human. I guess to some, ignorance truly is bliss!

The same principle applies to the "vanishing" ghost lady of Redcliffe. Visitors believe she is gone, because they can no longer see her. As one visitor told it, "I was so shocked when I saw her, she vanished before I could get my camera out!"

Unbeknownst to them, the ghost lady had continued down the staircase to check out these visitors to her home.

Another explanation offered by observers, after rubbing their eyes in disbelief, is "Maybe I imagined the ghost. Yeah, that must be it—my imagination is playing tricks on me!"

But not so! If they only had been able to talk to some of the many other witnesses who had seen this apparition over the years, their doubts would have been allayed. The ghostly lady of Redcliffe does indeed exist.

I myself saw her the afternoon Christen and I took the Redcliffe tour. We had no sooner stepped through the large front doors into the cavernous main hall when the ghost appeared at the head of the stairs. Resting her slender, pale hand on the stairwell, she leaned over it and exclaimed, "Oh, guests! We have some guests!" She bade us, "Welcome, welcome to Redcliffe."

Ever the gracious hostess in life, even death could not come between her and this ingrained training. She gracefully descended the staircase and then, once at the bottom, paused to observe us. As she studied us, she stood erect with a mantle of calm reserve wrapped around her. One could tell she had been well schooled to maintain her poise no matter what the circumstances. Yet despite this poise, a look of surprise slipped across her face when she realized I was observing her back.

The ghost lady had a patrician air about her that the beautiful, lavender gown she was wearing only accentuated. At ease with being so attractive, a sharp, curious intellect shone from her observant, hazel eyes. Everything about the ghost's demeanor spoke of having possessed wealth and privilege while alive. Yet despite this confident demeanor, an air of heavy sadness and regret hung around her that even the wealth could offer no balm for.

Who's she? I wondered, as so many had before me.

Reading my thoughts, the gracious ghost answered, "My name is Katherine Hammond Billings. I am the granddaughter of James Henry Hammond. Redcliffe is my home."

Not to be outdone in the good-manners department (after all, my mother *is* a real stickler for good manners!), I introduced myself. "I'm Boo Newell. People have told me how beautiful Redcliffe Plantation is. So, I came to see it for myself. I must say the descriptions don't do it justice. It's a beautiful place."

At my heartfelt compliment, Katherine's reserved demeanor warmed up some. I caught a gleam of mischief in her steadfast eyes when she teased me with, "Boo! What an unusual moniker! You didn't scare someone to get it, did you? You don't look so scary to me."

This last was said with such a sly, mischievous tone in the ghost's voice, I couldn't help but laugh with her. It was almost as if she knew what my family and friends know about me—that a tired, hungry Boo makes a grouchy Boo, which can be a scary Boo indeed!

Just then, Liza finished the tour introduction. Beckoning Christen and me to follow her to the next tour location, she unintentionally interrupted Katherine and me before we could finish talking. I asked Katherine if she would talk to me later.

"Of course, my dear," she graciously obliged. "It has been many years since I have talked to a living person. And you appear to be a most unusual and interesting one at that."

Having given her assent, she turned away and glided off to another part of her large home. I myself had to hurry to catch up with fast-walking Liza. She led us to the room that was off to the side of the main hall. This room was where I had earlier seen an older, male ghost peering out at us upon our arrival. He had frowned at our intrusion and then abruptly disappeared. Could he be the male specter from the mid-1800s era that had been seen over the years?

Who is he? I wondered.

I was about to get my answer. As we walked into the bedroom, there he stood awaiting our arrival, and none too pleased about it. The room had a distinct chill to it that the main hall had not possessed. The ghost was dressed in the height of fashion of a gentleman from the Victorian era.

There was an air of arrogance and authority around the specter. I knew we were standing in the presence of none other than the ghost of James Henry Hammond, the original owner of Redcliffe Plantation.

To verify this, I asked Liza if this had been James Hammond's bedroom when he was alive.

"Why yes it was, but how did you know?" she asked in puzzlement.

Now, I didn't respond with the old cliché "A little bird told me," as there was obviously no bird in the room to listen to. I said something to the effect that Hammond's energy was still strong in here. Christen looked at me and choked back her laughter, for of course it was still strong. The source of it was standing not six feet away, once again glowering at us in extreme irritation.

He was aware I could see him and this only added to his ire. Ignoring him for the moment, I turned my back on him to listen to Liza tell us about the room's artwork and furnishings. As I listened, I couldn't help but remember what I had learned in the visitor's center about the bedroom's former owner.

Hammond, when alive, had been a complex, controversial individual in the political and social life of pre-Civil War South Carolina. He had been a powerful and prosperous man and therefore someone those weaker didn't dare oppose. Hammond had not always been powerful and prosperous, though. He had been born on November 15, 1807. His parents, although hardworking people, never seemed to be able to get ahead in life. Lack of money was a perpetual source of concern, and so they always lived on the borderline of poverty. Young Hammond grew up jealous of everyone who had more than his family did. He was always conscious of the difference between he and others as far as dress and social standing.

Therefore, as Hammond grew to adulthood, he became determined to succeed at any cost, mostly at someone else's. He developed into a patronizing, ambitious, and egomaniacal adult. It came as no surprise to anyone, then, when in 1831, he courted and married an innocent young heiress named Catherine Fitzsimmons.

The sixteen-year-old Catherine was smitten with her new husband. But it soon became apparent to all that the only thing Hammond was smitten with was her huge dowry. His young bride brought to the marriage a large plantation called Silver Bluff. It came with 7,500 acres and 147 slaves. In return, Hammond brought nothing but his habitual arrogance and disdain, especially toward women. In fact, something he was fond of saying to his sons and anyone else when the subject of women came up was, "There are three things women are useful for. They were made to breed, serve as toys for recreation, and bring men wealth and position."

With this one calculated, marital stroke by marrying Catherine, Hammond had solved his problem of always lacking funds. Another benefit of the marriage was that it raised his social standing, guaranteeing his acceptance into the ranks of South Carolina's wealthy planters. These individuals owned the big land parcels, and the slaves to work them. They ruled the state as its "agricultural aristocrats."

Life should now have been good for Hammond and his wife and family.

Instead, because of his controlling personality and chronic dalliances with many women over the years, both slave and white alike, it was a miserable alliance for Catherine. Throughout their married life, she found herself an unwilling witness to her husband's many affairs. Most were of a transitory nature, but two that Hammond engaged in were of many years' duration and therefore a constant source of heartache to Catherine.

One of these affairs was with a slave woman named Sally. Hammond had bought eighteen-year-old Sally and her one-year-old daughter Louisa in 1830, before he married the then-clueless Catherine. He made Sally his mistress and fathered several children by her. When her daughter Louisa turned twelve, he had sexual relations with her while he was involved with her mother. Louisa also bore him several children.

Hammond's wife and slave women were not the only ones to suffer from an association with him. He was opinionated and bullying with family, friends, and enemies alike. This overbearing attitude made him unpopular with everyone. He always seemed to be able to quite effortlessly create enemies among his peers, who would then go out of their way to block his path to success. Because of his self-sabotaging actions, his best efforts to succeed at relationships, politics, farming, or any other endeavor he attempted were doomed to fail. Was it his fault when they failed? From his narcissistic point of view, of course not! To him, he was always the hapless victim.

Hammond wore this mantle of victimhood with great righteousness throughout his life. Blinded by this self-imposed victimhood, he was unable—or unwilling—to see the true reality of any situation, therefore thwarting himself from possibly rectifying it for the better. He thus lived his life in a vicious cycle of trauma and drama of his own making. It didn't help that the man possessed not a shred of patience nor understanding for anyone else's foibles but his own.

An example of the self-made trauma and damage to others that Hammond created occurred when it was discovered that he had molested four of his young nieces, the daughters of Catherine's sister. Instead of accepting responsibility for his actions and the resulting scandal, he blamed the girls' father for the irreparable damage done to their reputations. Their father, instead of keeping quiet, had gone after Hammond. Hammond reasoned that if their father hadn't raised a stink about their molestation in an attempt to make him pay, polite society wouldn't have found out about it. As it was, "the bird escaped from the cage," and the family scandal became common knowledge. Because of the moralistic attitudes of the times, the scandal damaged the girls' reputations so badly, no man ever asked for their hands in marriage. All four sisters remained unmarried their whole lives.

Hammond's family and friends were not the only ones to suffer because of an association with him. What of his lowly slaves? They were at the whims of their egomaniacal master. Yet he always saw himself as the victim in their master/slave relationship, never them. Why, wasn't he the one who always suffered when they died of ill treatment or overwork? When some of his male slaves died from fever after being forced to work on a weak dam in the middle of a horrific thunderstorm, who really suffered? Why Hammond did, right in the pocketbook. They had let him down, the rascals! Wasn't he the one who had had to go to the slave market and shell out his hard-earned money for replacements?

As for the living quarters for these unfortunate people, why go to too much trouble and expense to make them comfortable? The slave quarters were to serve merely as shelters, otherwise the inhabitants were to be out working. The slave cabins on Hammond's plantations, Silver Bluff and Redcliffe, were comprised of one room split into two small ones. Into these two rooms were crammed ten to twenty people, or two families. They contained no cubby holes, closets, or lofts, meaning there was no privacy. It also meant that Hammond, not trusting his enslaved workforce, could walk in at any time unannounced and see that nothing dangerous had been hidden from him. To be fair, most of the other plantations had similar living arrangements for their slaves.

Slave cabin at Redcliffe Plantation

But what about Hammond's slave women? Because of his enormous sexual appetite and proclivities, he found no satisfaction with his weak, unloved wife. So to satisfy himself, he turned to the women who didn't dare deny him: his female slaves. After all, didn't they exist for his pleasure? Didn't all women?

Yes, in life, James Hammond had been the epitome of an egomaniacal, controlling, manipulative individual. From the menacing, angry looks he was giving us now it was obvious he hadn't changed much, if at all, in death. The only difference was that here in the Ghost Realm he had no true power like he had once wielded in life. Did he know this? I would have to find the answer to this question later, for Liza, much to the ghost's satisfaction, was preparing to lead us to another part of the house.

As we walked out of his bedroom, I could feel Hammond's eyes and nasty energy bearing down on my back. Sensing this, Christen turned to me with a knowing grin. "I don't think you made a good impression on our host."

"Just wait till later. I'll make even more of an impression on him!" I shot back.

From behind me I heard a muttered "Good riddance!" in response.

After seeing James Hammond, that "later" couldn't come soon enough for me. Although Liza was a most informative guide, I was more eager to engage the ghosts of Redcliffe to get their stories than to know how many bathrooms the place had. In fact, there was one of the ghosts now whose story I was dying to get.

The ghost was Katherine Hammond, graciously beckoning us to ascend the grand staircase as we stood at the bottom of it. She must have done this many times while alive, for here she was in death still playing the hostess.

As we reached the top, she smiled at us and then turned away to enter a room off to the right. When I peered in I could see her giving directions to a ghost maid. There was a young male ghost in another one of the bedrooms, but he paid us no mind. I did likewise as Liza moved us along at a good pace.

After seeing the upstairs part of the house, she took us to see its outbuildings. There, in the stable, was the ghost of a black groom, one of the slaves from the 1800s. He was absorbed in the task of cleaning a brown English saddle. To one aware of the otherworldly activity around the old place, it appeared that Redcliffe Plantation was still in operation.

The key word here is "otherworldly."

In truth, nothing was getting done around the place anymore, at least not in the Earth Realm. So why were the ghost groom and other slave ghosts still "working" around Redcliffe? What was holding them trapped? Or maybe I should be asking *who*. Could the answer lie with the fact that the ghost of their overbearing master, James Hammond, was still trapped here himself, someone to be feared? This was one of the questions I was going to attempt to find the answer to later.

Later came sooner than I expected. As another tour group came across the lawn, Liza told us she had to go meet them but that we were free to explore the grounds on our own. Being more interested in who was inhabiting them rather than the buildings themselves, we made a beeline to the front veranda of the house. Christen sat on a rocking chair to relax and enjoy the beautiful, scenic view. I sat on the wooden bench by the front door to write in my investigation journal and check out a different scenery, ghosts. I didn't have long to wait.

As I was writing with my head bent down over my journal, the screen door to my right creaked open and then slammed shut. With firm footsteps, the ghost of James Hammond walked to my side. Bristling with antagonistic authority, it was obvious he wasn't happy to see me still here. He was accustomed to humans being around, but they were rarely ever aware of his ghostly presence. He didn't have to worry about them. With me, something was different. For one thing, I could see and hear him.

Standing over me now, he looked down upon me as an inferior interloper. As I continued to write (because I have to get the messages and impressions down as I receive them), I could feel Hammond's irritation growing at my refusal to instantly acknowledge his "important" presence. When glowering at me didn't work, he cleared his throat in a bid to gain my attention. It was evident what an impatient, demanding human he had been while alive from how he was now behaving as a ghost. I finally acquiesced to his impatience, looking up with a smile.

I needed to avoid antagonizing him further because I wanted to shift the energy between us to a higher vibrational level. Hammond didn't return my smile, though, instead querying aggressively, "Now look here, young woman, why have you come to my home?"

I noticed with hidden amusement that he had intentionally left out the more respectful term "lady" when addressing me. Well, I was dressed and acting unladylike by early 1800s standards. Also, even though I didn't mean it to be taken as such, Hammond felt threatened by my show of strength as evidenced by my refusal to be intimidated by his overbearing manner. Only men were meant to be strong and forceful, at least to Hammond's way of thinking. To him, women were meant to be predictable because of their "inherent" weak natures. I was obviously neither weak nor predictable, and it threw the ghost off his stride.

Giving me no time to answer his question as to who I was, he impatiently asked again, "Who are you? What do you want? You weren't invited here!"

Ignoring his brusqueness, I calmly answered back, "Hello James, my name is Boo."

Taking immediate umbrage with my familiarity with his name, the ghost chastised me. "You are too forward!

You're to address me as Mr. Hammond! Only my family and friends are allowed to call me James. You are neither!"

Well, let's get right to sword's point! I thought to myself (or at least, I believed I had).

I'd forgotten that Hammond, like all spirits, could easily read minds. He quickly shot back with the short, forceful reply: "Yes, let's! Then you will leave!"

"No, I won't!" I responded just as forcefully.

When dealing with a ghost as overbearing and narcissistic as this individual, it's not wise to appear weak. Even now, in death, he was still coming across as he had in life: drunk and delusional with his great power over others. Hammond still believed he had this power; didn't his mansion prove it? After all, hadn't he built Redcliffe to be a statement and monument to his success and power in life?

At my firm refusal to obey his command, I could see his arrogance slip. He simply didn't know what to do with me. The usual bullying tactics he had used in life weren't working on me. I obviously wasn't impressed by him, and I didn't scare easily. As a result, he was now waiting with a little more patience for me to explain myself further. It was time to disabuse him of some of the illusions he had about himself that he was still operating under.

"You can't order me off the premises as you could have in life. You're not of my realm anymore, the earthly one, so you have no power and control over me or any other human now. You're now the one who's the interloper!" I patiently but emphatically stated. I say patiently for I was trying not to come across as rude and disrespectful, yet still wanted to exude the firmness mixed with love needed to handle this recalcitrant spirit. When working with ghosts, it's all about balance. Otherwise, he might get offended and refuse to cooperate with me. He'd then be the one energetically controlling the direction of our encounter. The result might be that I wouldn't be able to help him and the other spirits trapped here.

Many of the slave ghosts were still trapped here because of him. As it had been in life, they were still too fearful of harsh retribution from the "master" to "run away" or "leave the plantation," to move out of the Ghost Realm and cross over. Their fear of James Hammond was the main issue trapping them in the Ghost Realm.

As I mused over the ghost slaves' plight, I could tell that James's slight patience wasn't going to last much longer. I could feel his edgy energy already starting to resurface as he waited for me to continue. So, getting our conversation back on track, I asked him, "Why are you still here?"

"This is all mine!" he stated with a sweep of his arm to include the vast landscape. "I must look after it!"

"You're no longer needed to look after it because it's no longer yours," I told him.

"Yes, it is! Without me Redcliffe is nothing."

"No," I responded, "without Redcliffe you feel that you are nothing!"

He stared at me, stunned. It was a novel notion to the ghost that he and the house and land were no longer one. I could sense his confusion growing. Suddenly feeling his vulnerability, the ghost looked away from me, refusing to meet my honest, steady gaze. Instead, he walked over to a nearby rocker and sat down.

What is the issue, the dilemma that is causing this confusion that has trapped him in the Ghost Realm? I wondered.

Ah, that's it, fear and despair! Before James Hammond died on November 13, 1864, at the age of fifty-seven, he had seen everything he had manipulated and worked for his whole life destroyed by the American Civil War. His powerful, privileged way of life lay about him in ruins. The Southern aristocracy was no more. Everything he had defined himself by was gone. This way of life had given him his so-called right to power of life and death over other human beings, namely his slaves. This prestige and power also justified to him his right to treat others ruthlessly and callously. Always so sure and opinionated in life, Hammond now didn't know what to do with himself in death.

Trying to break the stalemate between us, I asked Hammond once again, "Why are you still here? Redcliffe is no longer your true home."

This time, the stubbornness came more from fear than arrogance. "Yes, it is!"

"Have you never heard of the Other Side, the place that is called Heaven by the Christian religion and other religions?"

"Yes, of course I have!" he stridently answered, starting to puff up at the imagined inference that he wasn't a good, God-fearing man.

You were, according to your own skewed definition, I thought to myself, or at least I thought I did. For, once again overhearing my innermost thoughts, he shot back with, "Who are you to be judging me if you think you're so holy yourself!"

"Touché!" I told him with an appreciative laugh at my own hypocrisy. "Well said."

Hammond had unintentionally reminded me of the Bible verse "Judge not lest ye be judged." I always try to apply this when working with ghosts. After all, kindness should be exercised not only when dealing with one's fellow humans, but also spirits. Hammond had also demonstrated the validity of the advice I give to others before they do an investigation or clearing: "Be careful of your thoughts and judgments because the ghosts can hear them."

The reason for being careful is not only to make sure you exercise compassion for them, but also because they'll pick up on your attitude toward them from these thoughts. Are you fearful, contemptuous, judgmental, compassionate? Your attitude will come out and they'll usually respond likewise to you.

At my amused, self-deprecating laughter, Hammond started to relax. I realized that this spirit, deep down, had been worried that I would judge him to be a failure, just as he would have judged himself, and feared others would, if he hadn't possessed the accoutrements and trappings of wealth and power.

Just then, the ghost of a little slave boy of about nine materialized to our right. He walked up to Hammond's side and diffidently stood there. Fearful respect mixed with trepidation was written all over his young face. He was scared of his master, but he had an errand to do. What was it?

"Who's this little boy?" I asked.

Hammond carelessly responded, "He's nothing."

Once again I asked the question, but this time addressed it to the ghost child. He refused to answer me, though, first looking to Hammond for permission to speak. Seeing that I was going to persist, Hammond waved his hand in resigned assent.

"My name is Paul. I worked in the stables with my daddy, Ben. He got the fever and died one winter."

"That's enough, boy!" Hammond said curtly before he could say more about his father's mistreatment. "I had to have your daddy whipped for impertinence. Don't make the same mistake he made."

Paul grew silent, quickly stepping back and shrinking once again into his fear. I felt suddenly angered by Hammond's bullying of the little ghost. Just because you shouldn't judge a ghost doesn't mean you can't be firm with them when appropriate.

"You're no longer a slave, Paul," I said. "James Hammond controlled you in life—don't allow him to control you in death, for he can't. You're now free!"

Giving him an encouraging grin, I beckoned him over to me (I do confess to having a soft spot for ghost children). With the resiliency and hopeful spirit of the young at heart, the little ghost grinned mischievously back at me in delight and, giving the now-scowling Hammond a wide berth, skipped over to sit by my side.

As I turned my attention back to Hammond, the screen door opened and out glided the ghost of Katherine Hammond to join us, as she had promised to do earlier. She was a lady of her word. Knowing that one more ghostly addition would now add on to our time spent at Redcliff, I turned to Christen and asked her if she was okay with waiting a little longer to leave. Giving her assent, she returned to her patient repose.

Overhearing me, the always observant Katherine pointed a slim, white finger at Christen and asked me, "Who's she?"

"She's a good friend of mine who has a kind heart, like you do."

The gracious ghost beamed in delight at my sincere compliment. James, meanwhile, continued rocking away in the rocker, harrumphing now and then over our "lady's chatter," as he called it. Ignoring James's displeasure, I now gave Katherine my full attention. For, despite Katherine's lighthearted reaction to our exchange, she still had the deep, melancholy energy around her that I had noticed earlier. It surrounded her being like a permanent, heavy mantle.

What had happened in her earthly life to cause this depression? A depression so deep it had followed her into the Ghost Realm. *Why not just ask her?* I thought. I have found that the best way to usually get an honest answer from someone is to take the direct, honest route.

So I asked the beautiful ghost, "You seem so sad. What happened in your life to make you so?"

"I never felt understood and loved just for me," she answered with a weary sigh. "I had beauty, wealth, and position. Many men courted me, but none were good enough for my family. I fell in love with one of these young men. He was a fine, kind man, and we were talking marriage. My family disapproved of the match, though, so my father convinced me that the right and proper thing to do was to go away to school, to get an education.

"I now realize they sent me away not to get an education, but in the hopes that I would find a proper husband. I was sent to Boston to attend nursing school. It was so different from the life I had been used to at my dear Redcliffe. Here I felt loved and safe and happy. I didn't have to pretend to be someone else to fit in. In Boston, I was so lonely and homesick for Redcliffe and my family all the time. I was miserable.

"Life had been so much simpler here. But what was I to do? I didn't want to let my family down. I tried hard to succeed, but finally I gave up and came home. But there was one last way to redeem myself with my family. While I was at school, I had met a man named John Sedgwick Billings. He was a physician whose background and social standing were more to my family's approval. After a tumultuous courtship we became engaged and then married."

A shadow passed over the ghost's face. She now paused in her narrative in a vain attempt to control the sadness and regret creeping into her voice. With a sigh, she continued. "Shortly after the wedding, I realized I had made a grievous mistake. The love I had thought was there for me, and that I had hoped to build a happy marriage on, was an illusion. John didn't love me. It soon became apparent that I was nothing more to him than an attractive, proper wife to bear his children. I was constantly reminded of this fact by the numerous extramarital affairs he engaged in during our twenty-eight turbulent years of marriage. Ours was a loveless union.

"How could I have naively expected any more from it, though, when it had resulted from a loveless, troubled courtship right from the beginning? I should have seen how John was before I married him. I wouldn't see this at the time, though, because I was so intent on making my family and everyone else happy and proud of me."

Once again the ghost paused in her narrative, trying to wipe away the tears now streaming down her pale, translucent face with the back of a slim hand. These tears came from her sad memories of the past with its regrets and deep unhappiness.

Katherine had died relatively young at fifty-eight years old from chronic heart and thyroid conditions. Perhaps if she had lived longer she would have gained some life-sustaining wisdom: the wisdom that you can't, and shouldn't, try to make everyone else happy at the expense of your own well-being. If this is the road someone chooses to travel, then they'll never know true, lasting happiness and peace. This is because they're not being true to, and accepting of, who they truly are. Who they are is a beautiful, special, Divine being, worthy of nothing less than the best, whether it be in relationships, careers, etc. Once the person accepts this truism, they realize that they need, and are deserving of, nothing but the best for their own well-being.

Katherine hadn't realized this truth about herself while alive. This lack of understanding was now contributing to the issues that were holding her soul trapped in the Ghost Realm. To help her understand these issues so that she might resolve them, I needed her to finish her lapsed narrative. "Was there ever a time when you were happy?" I asked her. "Did nothing good come of your marriage?"

"The only good I received from my marriage was my three sons, one of whom died in childhood. They were my blessings and my salvation throughout the years. It was for them that I stayed with their father. The other thing that made my marriage bearable was my beloved Redcliffe."

Ah, now we're getting to the role that Redcliffe continues to play in what is keeping Katherine's soul trapped in the Ghost Realm, I thought. The old plantation home had some kind of hold over her trapped spirit. What was it? With her next words, the ghost told me.

"John and I resided in Woodstock, New York. Because of the strife between us, ours was a cold, unfeeling household. As a consequence, I returned to my beloved Redcliffe every chance I could. Here I always felt welcome and free, loved by the old house and land. I could be myself."

With these words the ghost lady momentarily forgot my presence as she gazed fondly around at Redcliffe's grounds spread out as far as the eye could see. Trying to draw her attention back to me, I asked her, "Katherine, are you aware that you're no longer of the Earth Realm?"

"Why of course, my dear Boo!" she responded with a chuckle of amusement and slight condescension. "How could I not be, what with the living calling me a ghost to my face? Oh, of course they don't know I can hear them. You know how obtuse and dense spirits can be when they're in their human forms." She laughed at her own witticism over the double meaning of the word "dense." I couldn't help but laugh with her, for of course we humans are denser because we exist in an energetically denser realm, the physical of the Earth Realm.

Being of a somewhat mercurial temperament, though, the ghost's mood shifted quickly back to serious and melancholic. In a tone of umbrage she stated, "Why, the way humans talk about me, you would think I was some kind of monster instead of what I am, a spirit like them! There are many other spirits on the grounds here, ghosts like Grandfather James, Paul, and me."

At the mention of his name, James stirred off to my side. In a gruff, impatient voice, he said, "Ladies, if you please!"

Glancing over at him, I acknowledged his bid for attention. "Just a minute, James. We'll be with you shortly."

As I turned away from his displeased frown, I couldn't help smiling. In a short while the ghost would have more attention than he'd bargained for! The time of decision for these spirits on whether to cross over was rapidly approaching.

This approaching deadline was becoming more and more apparent as the air around us began to feel lighter and lighter. This light, etheric energy belonged to the assembling higher beings, the angels. I couldn't see them yet, but I could feel their powerful, Divine energy nonetheless. The atmosphere around us was charged with it. I was reminded as to why I always find angelic energy so magical and magnetic—it's so powerful and strong yet so gentle, warm, and comforting, a combination and balance that not many other beings are able to master.

Katherine hadn't noticed the changing energy around us yet. She was now continuing her narrative in a strident tone of voice, as if in justification of her ghostly existence. "We all have our good reasons for staying on at Redcliffe!"

Ah, just the opening I had been waiting for to help her get some understanding of her true situation. This understanding would aid me in helping her cross over into the Light. "Why are you still here at Redcliffe trapped in the Ghost Realm, Katherine?" I asked. "What is your reason?"

"I love this house and it loves me. Nowhere else have I known such love. We understand each other."

"Have you ever thought about crossing over to the Other Side, Heaven as you would call it?"

"Yes, but I don't know what awaits me there," she said. "Just like I didn't know what awaited me in my marriage. Here I know what awaits me, what I have."

The ghost was beginning to get upset at the direction our conversation was taking. Firmly but gently I told her, "You have nothing here, Katherine, like you had nothing in your marriage. On the Other Side you will have everything you ever dreamed of having in your physical life: love, respect, understanding, complete acceptance for who you are, everything. The one thing you won't have is judgment. You will be loved unconditionally by the Divine.

"By clinging to this house for emotional security and to define your value as a person, you have kept yourself trapped in the Ghost Realm. You have traded true spiritual freedom for an illusion, the illusion that love awaits you nowhere else but here. This is not true. Even greater, truer love than is found in the Earth Realm awaits you on the Other Side. Can you not feel this great love for you from these angels around us?"

I paused to give Katherine time to become aware of the assembled angels patiently waiting by the doorway to the Other Side. James, meanwhile, was studying us with interest. He was beginning to catch a glimmer of something hopeful in our conversation, but it still wasn't quite tangible to him yet. He continued to listen as I resumed—or *tried* to resume—my conversation with Katherine.

At the sudden sight of the angels, she had gasped and gazed in wonderment at the bright, colorful lights shimmering all around them. Twice I had to say her name before I regained her attention. "Katherine, it's time for you to cross over, along with your grandfather James and Paul. You have been trapped long enough in the Ghost Realm. By staying in it, you're perpetuating the sterile, unhappy existence you lived in the Earth Realm, not replacing it with something better."

"Do you speak true?" she asked in a mixture of skepticism and hope.

Just then, loved ones came through the portal, excitedly calling to Katherine in greeting and answers. "Yes, she speaks the truth! You need to come with us," they said. "It's time. It's your decision, but if you will come with us to the Other Side you will find everything there you dreamed of having while alive. There's so much love there, and no judgment. It doesn't matter who you were or how much you had or didn't have in life. You're loved for yourself."

James interrupted the group to ask, "What awaits me there if I leave Redcliffe? I have done bad things while alive in the physical. How will I protect myself against retribution? I will have no power there, will I?"

I sensed some residual resistance from the ghost over releasing Redcliffe, his illusionary symbol of power and importance. "James, you have no real power here in the Ghost Realm. It's time for you to let this illusion go. You don't need Redcliffe to feel important and worthy and protected on the Other Side. You just are!"

"Yes, but I will be judged and punished for the things I did while alive."

"No, you won't. You won't receive punishment on the Other Side, only love. The Divine is merciful and knows your true heart, even if you don't. You will gain true power and peace from understanding why your life played out as it did. It's time for you to go Home now."

As James continued to ponder which course of action to take, to cross over or stay, Paul, the little slave ghost, got up off the bench. With an angel at his side, he fearlessly walked over to James and held out a small, brown hand, asking him, "Would you take me Home, Mr. James?"

James at first recoiled from the boy's overture. But when Paul smiled up in childish trust at the big, gruff ghost towering over him, a warm, soft glow spread across James's face. The big, redheaded angel waiting next to Paul smiled benevolently at both ghosts. He knew that the necessary, Divine energetic transformation of both lost souls had begun. Sure enough, James, with no hesitation at all now, held out a large, powerful hand toward the little boy, who grasped it trustingly.

"Come on, Paul. It's time to go Home!" James said, protectively leading the little ghost toward the glowing, golden Light. With the big angel leading the way, former slave and slave owner, now joined hand in hand in equality as they had always been in the eyes of the Divine, stepped into the Light and were gone.

One more ghost to go. Was she ready? I turned to where she stood at my side. Tears of happiness streamed down Katherine's face. She had decided to accept the peace and joy awaiting her on the Other Side.

Gesturing to the beautiful, waiting angels surrounding us, I asked her, "Katherine, are you ready?"

"Yes, Boo," she answered simply. But then a shadow momentarily crossed her face as remnants of the great loneliness she had felt in her physical life resurfaced. I could tell she still feared being alone, even on the Other Side. Sure enough, she asked me, "Will you come with me, Boo?"

"No, Katherine," I responded gently. "I can't go with you on this journey. Although my time of transition will come one day, it's not my time yet. You don't need me to come with you anyway, for you will not be alone, now or ever. Even while alive you, like all spirits in the physical, were never alone, for your deceased loved ones and guides and angels were always around you, loving you and watching over you. All under the loving auspices of the Divine."

As if to validate my reassurances to Katherine, movement at the entrance to the Light drew my attention. There, standing inside the Light, was the figure of a young man smiling and holding out his hand toward her. I couldn't see him clearly but obviously she could, for she lit up with joy. Clapping her hands in excitement and delight, she turned to me and exclaimed, "We do get second chances, Boo, we do! How marvelous!"

With that, Katherine eagerly turned back, walked to the Light, and grasped her young man's outstretched hand. Then, with no hesitation at all, she stepped into the Light and was gone.

And so Katherine, after all her fruitless, lonely years of haunting Redcliffe in search of love and peace, had found her way back to where they had been all along: her true Home, the Other Side. It had been just that simple!

OLD CAHAWBA: A TRUE GHOST TOWN

Cahawba. The name rolls rather easily off the tongue. The problem is, old Cahawba rolled just as easily off the map and out of existence. This, even though it was the first state capital of Alabama.

The state of Alabama itself was established on December 14, 1819, becoming the twenty-second state in the young country. The new state was created from lands appropriated from the Creek Indians after they lost the Creek War of 1813–1814. Cahawba was founded in 1819 to be the new state's permanent capital. The "permanent" part turned out to be only in theory, not in fact. The early planners of old Cahawba had not put much forethought into its location. Or, to use an expression of the time, "They lacked horse sense."

They established the city at the confluence of the Alabama and Cahaba Rivers. At the time it seemed to be an ideal location. Yet Cahawba's location turned out to be a classic case of enthusiasm overriding common sense. It was ideal only for the myriad number of mosquitoes infesting the area. They now had a new bumper crop of hosts to hunt and feed on. Fever and death spread among the populace.

As if the swarms of hungry mosquitoes weren't enough, the land the town was built on was prone to frequent flooding. Within a short time of its birth, Cahawba gained a well-deserved reputation for being an unhealthy and dangerous place to sink your fortunes into. Talk began that the state capital needed to be relocated. The effort for relocation gathered momentum. Although the citizens of Cahawba fought this effort, it was in vain. There were too many factors working against them.

One of the main factors, besides the town's unhealthy location (which they tried to correct with drainage ditches of fast-flowing water), were the powerful political factions at work. Swarms (I do apologize to the mosquitoes for any comparison!) of politicians and speculators stood to reap great profits from a new state capital location.

So, in 1826, the state capital was relocated to Tuscaloosa. Eventually it ended up in Montgomery, which is still the state capital of Alabama today.

After it lost its function and importance of being the center of government for the state, Cahawba started to die. The population dwindled. Then came King Cotton in the early 1850s! A railroad line was built to accommodate the cotton flooding in from the surrounding plantations. Cahawba found itself resurrected as an important cotton port on the Alabama River. At one time, in fact, it was the fourth-richest city per capita in the young United States. The town seemed once again assured of becoming a thriving, wealthy area—an area whose survival and increasing wealth were now dependent on cotton and slaves.

Then came the Civil War in 1861. With Union gunboats blocking Mobile Bay farther down the river, there was no way to ship the cotton to important overseas markets. King Cotton was assassinated by strangulation. The town that had been given a second chance at life now found itself once again dying.

Despite the almost fatal blow of losing its cotton economy, Cahawba was still able to cling tenaciously to existence as the county seat. Then, in 1865, a devastating flood of massive proportions struck the area. The county seat was moved to nearby Selma, finally sealing Cahawba's fate.

People left the town in droves. Shop owners couldn't sell their businesses, so they simply closed them down and walked away. Homes were abandoned as their occupants fled the rapidly disintegrating town. Where once there had been a vibrant, hopeful population of between three thousand and six thousand residents in the early 1860s, by 1870 Cahawba's population had dropped to below five hundred.

Most of these remaining residents were freed slaves from nearby plantations. Even these freedmen eventually abandoned Cahawba to her inevitable downward spiral into obscurity. Once the freedmen left, the decline of Cahawba's once magnificent mansions, courthouse, churches, and other structures accelerated until all had vanished, victims of scrap dealers, neglect and decay, and the ever-advancing wilderness. All that's left now on the land where Cahawba once thrived are its two old cemeteries and markers informing the curious where certain structures once stood and events took place.

This dearth of living spaces doesn't deter one group of tenacious residents, though: ghosts! They're still living in, or rather *occupying*, Old Cahawba in death as they did in life. In fact, they find it downright hospitable. The sheer amount of ghosts and paranormal activity to be found at Old Cahawba bears testament to this. Once word spread among those in the Ghost Realm about the old ghost town, spirits flocked to it from miles around. Need unlimited sources of energy to plug into to recharge after a hard day of gliding around sightseeing? Old Cahawba's got 'em. Just go floating over the Alabama and Cahaba Rivers! How about a hospitable population of your own kind to welcome you and show you around? Old Cahawba's loaded with ghosts! What more could a confused, restless spirit wish for?

How about spiritual peace? This peace of the spirit is the one thing not provided at Old Cahawba. It can only be acquired and experienced after the ghost gains clarity and understanding about the issues that are anchoring it in the Ghost Realm.

I first heard about Old Cahawba not through the "ghost-vine," but in the more mundane way of another human informing me. A man named Tommy Becker had come on the Decatur Ghost Tour, the ghost tour I own and operate in Atlanta, Georgia. Tommy turned out to be an intrepid, experienced investigator of the paranormal. After the tour, he told me that although he was impressed with the evidence he had gathered on the tour, there was a location I needed to check out that was overrun with ghosts. Tired as I was after a long day of doing readings then the tour, my ears came to full attention.

"Where is this place?" I asked.

"It's Old Cahawba, located a few miles from Selma, Alabama," he said.

He then proceeded to tell me about the many happenings he had experienced while investigating the old ghost town. Some of the experiences involved the great electronic voice phenomena (EVPs) he and his fellow investigator, Celia, had captured at several of the locations on the grounds. EVPs occur when you capture the discarnate spirit's voice on your recording equipment. Tommy and Celia had also seen shadowy figures rushing by them and captured a couple of awesome apparitional camera shots of the ghosts themselves.

Okay! Old Cahawba and Boo would be a perfect match! I couldn't wait to check it and its denizens out. What—and *who*—would I find?

On the day I went to Old Cahawba I was accompanied by three of my best friends and kindred spirits, Beth Sullivan, Sami Glow, and Fay Newell. The latter just happens to be my mother. Now I can just hear you, my astute reader, thinking, *Oh right, gotta carry Mom along to keep you out of trouble!* Well, I'd respond to that with, Wrong! You've got it backward. I carry Fay along to get me into trouble!

Fay is one of the most adventuresome, free-spirited individuals I have ever had the pleasure to know. She is fun and has a great sense of humor, necessary attributes that came in handy while raising such an oddball, precocious child as I was. Okay, okay, I must admit I didn't leave this oddball child behind when I grew up. She's still a large part of what makes eccentric, adult Boo who she is today. And Mama Fay proudly takes some credit for my eccentricity. Although she didn't always understand my oddness as a child (it's no wonder, what with ghosts always floating through my bedroom and other unusual happenings), she always gave me free rein to be who I was, a very shy yet independent little girl.

Also, unlike me, Mom never meets a stranger, whether human or ghost. And good grief, she could have had a lucrative career as a therapist or spy. Within five minutes of being around her, the stranger has found themselves incapable of resisting the urge to spill all they know to her. Lucky for them, Fay is as good at keeping secrets as she is at listening to them! This is because she genuinely loves people.

There have been times on some investigations where someone hasn't felt comfortable opening up about their paranormal experiences. Then having Fay, the human information sponge, along comes in handy. Within the first five minutes, the person has disgorged their unsettling information to Fay, acquired a new friend, and I've got the information I need.

This is how it played out the day we arrived at Old Cahawba Archaeological Park. Before proceeding into the park, we stopped at the small visitor's center to get a map of the grounds. There, behind the counter, was a volunteer named Jacob Benson. He was available to help visitors understand the archeological significance of the park. His cohort was Kevin Johnson. The two men also served as dedicated caretakers of the old site. They worked under the direction of Linda Derry, the site director.

Linda is a well-known and highly respected archaeologist who has dedicated a large portion of her career and expertise to researching and saving Old Cahawba for present and future generations. In fact, Linda is so well known in the area for her championship of the old town, you might say she's its unofficial mayor. Of course, in all fairness, it must be pointed out she won the "election" by default. There was simply no one *alive* to run against her.

Jokingly, I asked Jacob if all the "citizens" were happy with Linda's term. Were there any complaints? Being a man of quick wit and a ready sense of humor, he quipped back with a laugh, "Haven't heard a single one from anybody. In fact, I haven't heard from anybody, period! So she must be doing a good job!"

Not only does Jacob have a good sense of humor, but he's also a gracious man. His easygoing manner, like my mom's, is guaranteed to put anybody at ease. He and Mom hit it off. And so, before Jacob knew it, he had launched into a recital of the many paranormal experiences witnessed at Old Cahawba.

He said the grounds the old town had stood upon could feel creepy at night. Another unsettling time could be the early evening when he's closing up the park for the day. Sometimes he would get the feeling that he was being watched. He'd quickly look around but there was no one there, at least no one he could see. Visitors reported hearing voices in conversation and seeing unexplained lights bobbing about the grounds. Many times visitors also reported hearing children's voices and laughter around them as they strolled through old New Cemetery. It was as if, maybe, there were children still playing there. Little did these visitors realize that it wasn't a maybe, but a fact! In actuality, there were children playing all around them. They just came in a different form than what most humans were used to seeing.

Jacob himself had had his own experiences with the ghost children as they played on their otherworldly playground. One sunny afternoon he'd taken his five-year-old grandson with him while making his rounds. They ended up at New Cemetery.

The cemetery had been created in 1851 to be Cahawba's more modern burial grounds. It had replaced Capital Cemetery, which had been laid out and established in the early 1820s. As the town reinvented itself as an important river port for cotton shipping, Capital Cemetery was no longer considered grand enough.

Jacob had been standing there watching his little grandson exploring and playing around one of the old graves. He said the little boy had been playing and talking like any normal five-year-old would. Upon closer observation, though, he realized his little grandson appeared to be playing and talking not by himself, but with someone or something else! Who or what, Jacob didn't know. His grandson had been playing next to a burial obelisk erected over the grave of a young boy named Benjamin Evans. Benjamin had been six years old when he died on September 11, 1856.

Benjamin Evans's epitaph in New Cemetery at Old Cahawba

When Jacob had called his grandson over to him, the little boy started asking questions about the children dying, what death is, what happens after you die, where you go, and other such deep questions. The two had moved on, talking about the subject of death as they walked—a most unusual subject of interest for a five-year-old to be dwelling on out of the blue.

Then the little boy had gotten distracted by a butterfly on a nearby bush. Forgetting the subject of death, he had raced off to check it out, leaving his puzzled grandfather behind to ponder what had stimulated the boy's sudden, fleeting interest in death. Jacob wouldn't get the answer until a few months later.

Every year on Halloween, the archaeological park runs haunted hayrides through the grounds of the old ghost town to raise much-needed funds. Jacob is responsible for the lighting. He was out one night before Halloween checking the lights before the nighttime tours started. All of a sudden, from out of the gloom and mist, came a little blue-gray shadow. It glided up to Jacob and stood by his right knee.

"Where's the little boy?" Jacob heard the small shadow ask.

Suddenly, he realized the shadow was the ghost of Benjamin Evans wondering where his little playmate, Jacob's grandson, was. Before Jacob could come out of his shock enough to respond to the little ghost, the shadow disappeared.

"What'd you do then, Jacob?" I asked him.

"Well, I've heard the ghost children laughing and playing in the cemetery before, but I have to admit it kinda spooked me to know that they were all around me in the dark, watching me, and I couldn't see them. Let's just say I didn't stay too long checking the lights!"

After listening to more of Jacob's stories of otherworldly occurrences witnessed by him and others around the park, I couldn't wait to meet Old Cahawba's ghostly denizens myself! The question was, would they want to meet me? I intended to find out posthaste!

Leaving the park office, we walked around the old ghost town to get a feel for its energy. Ghostly shadows could be seen flitting around and moving about their otherworldly business in the weak light thrown by the late-afternoon sun. The ghosts were definitely here, and in large numbers at that! Each one of the historic locations had its ghostly denizens. Even though the old town's buildings were no longer there, many of their former occupants still were! They were anchored to the former buildings' residual energies, which had been imprinted onto the grounds where the buildings had once stood.

After wandering around Old Cahawba for a while, we ended up at old New Cemetery. By this time Mom and Sami had gotten tired of following me around as I prowled through the grounds of the old town. They plopped down on the bench located at the entrance to New Cemetery, refusing to go further. Both assured me that they were happy to sit and relax as they enjoyed the peace and quiet of the old burial grounds.

It was maybe quiet to them, but to me it was quite a noisy place, what with all the ghost children playing and running around. These ghosts were the children who had once been alive in Old Cahawba when it had been a living, vibrant town. Now their ghosts were using the very cemetery their bodies had been buried in as their playground. They were chasing each other and screaming and shouting in glee. There were a few adult ghosts, presumably their parents, walking among them.

The happy, playful games of the ghost children appeared normal enough, but instead of playing on real playground equipment, they were using the old graves instead. They were playing tag and hide-and-seek among the weathered, leaning headstones. There was even a game of stickball going on, with the graves serving as bases. Who said an old cemetery couldn't be fun?

Well, enough of me just watching the young ghosts. It was time for me to join them! I entered the cemetery followed by intrepid Beth and her camera. I say intrepid because, although she can be apprehensive about some of the otherworldly locations we investigate, she'll still come along to make sure she doesn't miss some awesome camera shots. And so it was on this day.

Of course, the fact that I failed to mention at the time that there were ghost children playing all around us might have influenced her decision somewhat to come along. And I wasn't about to tell her that that blast of cold air she mentioned feeling had come from the little redheaded ghost boy who had run through her right leg as he ran away from the playmates chasing him! *Let her think that it was a cold breeze that had sprung up around her*, I thought.

So, in a shared spirit of exploration and adventure, we walked around the cemetery. Some of the young ghosts stopped their play to better observe us. What was the difference that set us apart from other visitors from the realm of the living who had come to visit the old cemetery? The answer came when a little ghost girl about ten feet away with curly, brown hair stopped playing tag to point at me and squeal excitedly, "Look at her, look at her! She's one of us!"

"No, she's not!" an older boy hollered back. "But she's different from the others who come. She can see and hear us!"

Ah, that was what was attracting their attention. They could feel my energy now vibrating on the same frequency as their ghostly energy. This shared frequency was what was facilitating our connection. I was also looking directly at them in a conscious way, denoting awareness of their existence.

As we continued to explore among the graves, trying to read the inscriptions carved into the old, moss-covered headstones, I could feel myself being drawn to a small hill on the other side of the cemetery. When we reached the hill we discovered an old stone obelisk. It was serving as a marker and monument over one of the graves in a family plot.

At one time, New Cemetery had possessed many such fine obelisks and funerary monuments to mark the final resting places of the town's citizens. But over the years, with no one living in the ghost town to stop the ever-invading wilderness, it had continued its relentless march to claim the cemetery grounds and its contents. The roots of trees that had grown up unchecked around the graves had cracked some of the slabs from underneath. At other graves the roots and erosion had caused the ground to fall away from the burial sites, opening them up to the elements. Bushes and weeds grew around and over other graves, obscuring them.

And as if this wild landscape wasn't enough of a challenge for the cemetery's caretakers, there were the vandals who had abused and exploited the old cemetery over the years. These were individuals who had been too shallow and callous to care about the consequences of their nefarious activities. They had stolen funerary art and headstones, and wantonly destroyed the graves themselves.

The spirits aren't the ones affected by this criminal activity, though. From what I've gathered from spirits who have moved on—*moved on* being the key phrase here—most of them are not that concerned with the condition of the space that contains the remains of the earthly vehicle they left behind, their physical body. That's because they now see this vehicle for what it always was, a temporary convenience (or inconvenience, depending on the life they lived) to help them accomplish their earthly mission.

The living are the ones adversely affected by vandalism when they visit the graves of their loved ones to connect with them and do research on ancestors. Dates, names, no more! The perpetrators must have forgotten that such desecration could be inflicted on their own final resting place. Then their earthly remains would also lie in an unmarked grave, lost to perpetuity.

As we approached the stone obelisk, I was relieved to discover that it had been relatively undisturbed by the passage of time and human activity. It stood in a family plot surrounded by other graves. I stooped down to read who was buried underneath such a fine monument. The inscription on the obelisk read:

Benjamin Evans
Born October 6, 1849
Died September 11, 1856
NONE KNEW HIM BUT TO LOVE HIM

What a beautiful, simple epitaph, I thought. There was such a poignancy and longing in it, it brought tears to my eyes. In the epitaph's simplicity, one could feel the depth of the grief experienced by the little boy's family over their great loss.

I now knew who was buried under the obelisk, but what about why was I drawn to it? Then, looking at Benjamin's birthdate once again, I was astounded to realize that the little boy and I shared the same birthday. I too had been born on October 6, just in a later century. Was there some energetic bond between us that transcended the intervening years? Had the spirit of Benjamin been calling out to mine through time on the chance that I could help him and his trapped loved ones?

As I pondered these questions, I suddenly felt a presence on my left. Turning around, I beheld the ghost of a little boy of about six observing me. He was dressed in a small, long-sleeved, white shirt and brown knee pants. His dark, curly hair was tousled from play. Realizing that I had noticed him, he shyly grinned as he approached to stand in front of me.

I could feel the joy emanating from his whole being that came from having the innocence of a young child. Looking up at me with this joy sparkling in his big blue eyes, he stalwartly held out a small, grubby hand for me to shake, saying, "Hi, my name is Benjamin."

What an inquisitive, enchanting little creature you are! I thought as I responded back, "My name is Boo. How do you do?"

I put my hand out to shake his, or at least attempt to. His small, pale hand didn't have the substance for me to grasp it in a genuine handshake. This didn't matter to the little boy, though; it was the intent that mattered. Looking positively delighted with how our exchange was going, he giggled over the simple rhyme I had made. The ice between us was broken.

Boo channeling Benjamin's story at Old Cahawba

I walked over to the old, cracked, concrete grave slab located beside the obelisk and sat down. The little ghost followed me over and sat on my left. We sat there for a moment in companionable silence, basking in each other's energy. I didn't know what he thought of mine, but his was positively wonderful! Finally, because we both possessed curious dispositions, we couldn't resist giving in to them.

"What's she doing?" He pointed a stubby little finger at Beth and her camera.

"It's called a camera, and she's taking pictures with it. It's just much smaller than the ones you're used to."

"What's her name? Can she see me?"

"Her name is Beth and no, she can't see you."

Giggling in merriment at the thought of being invisible to her, he turned back to me. "What are you doing here, Miss Boo?"

"I came to check out the ghosts of Old Cahawba and to see if any of these trapped spirits would like help moving on to their true Home, the Other Side."

The inquisitive little ghost quickly asked, "Where is this Home, Miss Boo? Who lives there?"

Trying to keep my explanation simple and understandable for this six-year-old, I answered, "This Home is what your family calls Heaven. It's where our loved ones go after they have died. It's the place spirits are supposed to return to when their physical bodies are no more. Some spirits get stuck, though, in a place called the Ghost Realm. This delays their return to their true Home where peace and love await them. These stuck spirits are the ones I try to help move on, go Home to the Other Side." Turning the attention back to him, I asked, "Why are you still here, Benjamin?"

With a mischievous grin, he exclaimed with a laugh, "It's fun! We can do anything we want to!"

Despite his merry laughter, I could tell that underneath he was troubled and confused by my explanation—and something else. I gently asked him, "Benjamin, are you aware that you have died? That you no longer have a physical body?"

"Yes, but what's dead?" he asked. "I can run and play!" With this statement, the energetic little ghost suddenly remembered that I'd interrupted his playtime. Exclaiming "I've got to go play!" Benjamin hopped off our grave slab and started to run back to his playmates.

So much for holding the attention of a lively six-year-old boy with more important things on his mind than the Spirit Realm! I thought with amusement.

But just before he ran off, he turned and hollered back at me, "You can come and play too, Miss Boo, but watch out for Chester! He's not nice. He pins us to the ground!"

Ah, the proverbial playground bully knows no time period, I thought.

Now, although I was flattered by Benjamin's invitation to come play, and yes, I do have fun playing with ghost children when I get the chance (they are, after all, like living children everywhere except for the lack of a physical body), I couldn't. My time in the cemetery was growing short because one of the caretakers would be arriving soon to lock it up for the night. With this in mind, I quickly called to the little ghost boy, "Wait Benjamin, please come back."

Full of restless energy but a polite child nonetheless, he reluctantly walked back to me. Sitting down on my right side, he scooted over to get close to me as I wrote in my notepad. Becoming curious, he moved even closer to watch me write. I could feel his cold, ghostly form numbing my right arm and elbow. Looking up at me with a mischievous light shining out of his bright-blue eyes, he excitedly informed me, "I'm gonna learn to write one day! But Mama said I have to pay more attention in school. Miss Alice told her I talk too much. I do like to talk!" he admitted with a giggle. His precocious, childlike energy reminded me of how I imagined Peter Pan's to be.

"Is Miss Alice your teacher?"

"Yes."

"Do you like her?"

"Oh yes, she's nice. All us boys like her. She's pretty!" he stated with all the enthusiasm of a first crush.

Just then the ghost of an attractive young woman glided up to us. Her long, brown hair was caught up in a bun at the nape of her neck.

Who is she? I wondered.

Hearing my thoughts, the ghost woman responded, "I'm Mrs. Evans, Benjamin's mother. He's a naughty boy and will not come home. I've been calling him and calling him!"

Looking apprehensively at his upset mother, Benjamin hurriedly stood up. I could hear him thinking, *I hope Mama's not mad at me!*

Even if she were, I knew it wouldn't last. Despite the obvious exasperation with her son, a great maternal love for the little boy shone brightly through the irritation. This great love wasn't the only emotion I picked up around Benjamin's mother, though. There was also great mental confusion and fear as well. Did she know she was dead? Obviously not, for she saw herself as she saw me: alive in the physical. Yet unlike my physical body, hers was an illusion. Another indication of her confusion as to which realm she was in was that to her, there had been no passage of historical time. She was still behaving as she had 158 years before the present time period.

Now I realized the true reason Benjamin didn't want to leave the Ghost Realm. He wouldn't go without his mother. He knew he was dead but didn't know what to do about it or where to go. This does happen now and then with ghost children when the adults around them who have passed are confused about their own true state of existence.

Such was the case with Benjamin and his mother. His mother was dead but didn't know it (it's a type of denial), so she was unable to help them return to their true Home. And how could he help her? How does a six-year-old tell his mother, an authority figure he's been raised to love, respect, and trust, that she is wrong about something? Especially something like death.

As I was thinking about Benjamin's dilemma, the ghost of a little blond girl of about his age suddenly ran by us. She ran to the old cedar tree at the corner of the family plot and hid behind it. I could see her fearfully peeking out at us, for she knew something different was going on.

I started to call the shy little ghost girl over to us but got distracted by Benjamin's still-panicked mother tearfully asking him, "Where have you been, Benjamin? I've looked all over for you!"

Trying to console her, little Benjamin took her hand, telling her, "Don't cry, Mama, don't cry. I'll be a good little boy, you'll see."

He was trying to comfort her now, just as he'd attempted to comfort her at the time of his death. At that time, now in his spirit form, he had tried to futilely hug his mother to console her as she mourned by his deathbed. Then, as now, there was still a deep sadness that clung heavily to the ghost mother. It was obvious that her grief in life over her young son's death had known no lessening with time. She had hopelessly mourned him till the day she died. Yet even then, her own death brought her no peace. Like any good, loving mother, she went looking for her child. She had found him playing around the family burial plot.

To her, because of her confused mental state from her great loss, she believed that she and her little Benjamin were still alive. For if they were dead, wouldn't she be separated from him once again, losing him for good? This the loving mother was determined not to let happen again! Her losing him once more was her worst fear.

Trying to help her gain some clarity as to the true state of her existence, I asked the ghost mother if she was aware that she was dead. Wiping her tears away with the back of a translucent hand, she indignantly stated, "I'm not dead! And neither is my little boy! How dare you say such a thing?"

Standing stiffly with slender hands clasped tightly in front of her, she presented a brave front. Yet one could feel the desperate fear of loss around her. She floated over to my left and, with billowing skirts, gracefully sat beside me. Once again I was enveloped in the heavy ghost cold. There was an edgy feel to her energy as she nervously arranged and rearranged the folds of her long, black mourning gown. Again, she emphatically stated that she and Benjamin were still alive. As she continued to refute and deny their deaths, I wondered who she was trying to convince, me or herself.

Just then, Beth walked up to inform me that all the ghostly energy was causing her camera to malfunction. Well, a ghost must get energy from somewhere, right? As Beth and I discussed the camera situation, I overheard Benjamin's mother ask him, "Who's she talking to? There's nobody there."

To her, Beth was invisible.

The ghost's refusal to acknowledge her death was preventing her from being able to get on the same energetic frequency as Beth's, that of a person still in an energetically heavier, physical body. She didn't know there was a difference.

Benjamin, because he had accepted that he was dead, could shift his energy back and forth so that he could see the living who visited the cemetery. The ghost mother was able to see me because I had shifted my energy to match the frequencies of the Ghost Realm.

The little boy, confused by his mother's inability to see what he saw, was slow to answer her question. She asked him once again, with growing impatience, who I was talking to. "There's no one there!" she said.

"Oh yes there is, Mama!" Benjamin said. "It's the other lady who came with Miss Boo."

Instead of believing what Benjamin told her, she rebuked him, saying, "There's no one there, Benjamin. You know it's not nice to tell lies!"

"I'm not, Mama! She's there with the shiny thing in her hand. It lights up."

The little ghost boy teared up at his mother's displeasure. I noticed that he was starting to look pale and wan from our interaction. Feeling sorry for the earnest little ghost, I told the ghost mother, "Benjamin is not lying! You can't see Beth, the other human here beside me, because you're dead and in denial about it. Beth is alive and in a different realm from the one you're in."

"What do you mean by that?" she asked, looking confused by my explanation.

Before I could answer, Benjamin interrupted, "Mama, when are we going home? I'm hungry."

"Any time now, Benjamin. We don't want to be rude to this nice lady."

I suppressed the urge to laugh in amusement at her polite description of me. Instead, I asked her where her home was.

"Down the street about four blocks from here," she said, pointing in the direction where one of the neighborhood areas of Old Cahawba had once stood. She obviously had no idea that her earthly home was no more. It was time to enlighten her about her and Benjamin's true state of existence so they would hopefully choose to move on.

Old Cahawba: a true ghosts' town

"Mrs. Evans, are you aware that your home, you, and Benjamin, as well as the whole town of Cahawba, are no longer in the physical realm?" I asked.

Visibly upset by my statement, she asked in sudden alarm, "What do you mean, we're not in the physical? I will not listen to such talk anymore! It's time for Benjamin and me to go home. And it's a fine one too, I might add! Mr. Evans will be coming home at any time and he expects his dinner to be ready. I have no more time to waste on this nonsense!" With that, the ghost mother stood, took Benjamin's hand, and turned to walk away.

"You have no real home to go back to!" I called after her. "What you think is your home is an illusion. Even the time period you're in is an illusion. Look at me, my clothes. Do I look like I belong in your time? No, because time has moved on! It moved on without you because you're not of the Earth Realm, the realm of the physically alive, anymore."

The ghost turned back, looking at me in growing agitation. Tears of fear welled up again in her eyes. It was time to call in some Divine aid. I sent out a quick plea to the angels and Mother Mary. They came immediately, as they always do in answer to prayer.

The angels were attired in different shades of beautiful, rich blues, greens, golds, reds, and more. Their raiment sparkled with golden and silvery lights. Mother Mary herself was clothed in a simple gown of the most beautiful royal purple. There was a warm, golden light that shown all around her from the powerful energy of unconditional love.

The ghost mother looked startled by the sudden appearance of these Divine beings. Not so Benjamin! He looked positively delighted! He ran over to get acquainted with a big, redhaired angel.

Ah, the faith of little children! I thought.

Pointing to Mother Mary, I asked the ghost mother if she knew who this lady was. She shook her head in silent negation. Before I could tell her, Mother Mary walked over to Benjamin's mother and held out her hands. Taking the ghost mother's hands in a tender grasp, she told her, "My name is Mary. I know the great grief that you feel, for I too am a mother. I too lost a beloved son to Death, or so I thought. But this wasn't so. Death is not eternal, only Life of the spirit is. You are not alive anymore in the physical realm, which is a temporary life for the spirit at the most. Only the Realm of Spirit is truly eternal, with no end. Your grief and fear have trapped you and your little boy in a place worse than Death. It's time for you both to come Home."

"But we have a home," the ghost mother timorously responded back.

"No, you don't. You're not of the physical earth any longer. Your physical home is no more. The passing years have destroyed it. The only home you have is waiting on the Other Side with the Divine. My Son is living proof that Death is temporary, not eternal. Only the spirit is eternal."

At Mother Mary's words, the Light, the doorway to the Other Side, opened to her left. At the sight of the beautiful, glowing doorway, the ghost mother began to cry. "I'm so tired!" she sobbed. "I'm so tired of trying to look after Benjamin to keep him safe and alive so I don't lose him again!"

"You don't have to anymore," Mother Mary reassured her. "That is what these angels are here for, to look after Benjamin and you also. All you have to do is take my hand and I will walk with you into the Light. There's nothing to fear, for Death cannot follow you and your little boy where you're going, to your true Home."

Still somewhat hesitant, the ghost mother reached out to touch my arm for comfort. She gave a startled gasp as her pale, ghostly hand passed through my solid forearm. "What is this? Who are you?" She pulled back in sudden alarm.

"My name is Boo and I'm of the earthly realm, the realm of the physically alive."

"Why can't I touch your arm?"

"Because my spirit is still in its physical body, while your spirit no longer has a body to inhabit."

"So the lady speaks the truth?" she asked, pointing to Mother Mary.

"Yes, it's true. You and Benjamin are dead in the Earth Realm."

"I don't want to lose him again!" she exclaimed in renewed anguish. "I will not!"

"Mrs. Evans, the only way to make sure of this is to take him into the Light. Mother Mary and the angels will make sure you and Benjamin cross over safely. Then you can be together for as long as you like."

Speaking of Benjamin, where was he at? Ah, there he was over beside the big, redheaded angel. He was fascinated with the angel's wings. The angel had lowered his great form down onto one knee to make it easier for the little boy to reach out and touch his soft, white wings. Benjamin was happily stroking and playing with them. Who could ask for a more perfect babysitter? They were giggling and laughing with so much glee that even the sad ghost mother was affected by it. Her whole demeanor began to relax and lighten up.

Mother Mary looked over at Benjamin's angel and gave him a knowing smile. It was as if a silent signal passed between them. The big angel stood up to his full great height, holding the little ghost boy tenderly in his arms. The time of crossing was at hand.

Seeing slight hesitation still on Mrs. Even's face, I told her, "You must go with them, Mrs. Evans. It's the only way. There will be children for Benjamin to play with. His father is also there waiting for you and his son."

As if on cue, a man with brown hair and a beard stepped out of the Light. There was a small, tan dog running around his feet.

"Ripper!" Benjamin screamed in glee. "Where have you been, boy? I've missed you so much!"

The little dog yapped happily at the sight of his boy. The angel handed Benjamin over to his father. Holding the boy in his arms, Benjamin's father eagerly walked over to his wife. Her hesitation and fear had evaporated, replaced by indescribable joy at the sight of her beloved husband. Quickly she slipped her arm through her husband's, hugging him tightly to her.

"Come on, love. It's time to go Home," he said gently.

With that, they turned and walked toward the Light, Benjamin wrapping his little arms around his father's neck. As they moved closer to it, the angels gathered around them. One of the angels moved up to walk beside Benjamin's father. The little boy, recognizing his redheaded friend, couldn't resist turning loose long enough to make a grab for one of those magical, soft, white wings. I wasn't able to see if he was successful, though, for just then they stepped into the bright Light and were gone. Even so, I could hear Benjamin and his angel laughing in merriment!

Mother Mary was the last to enter. But before she did, she paused and turned to look at something behind me. What was arresting her attention? I turned to look just in time to catch a glimpse of the little golden-haired girl once again ducking behind the tree. She had been watching us the whole time. Because of her shyness, though, she hadn't dared to join us. To my chagrin, I had forgotten all about her when I became involved with the plight of Benjamin and his mother.

Yet Mother Mary had not! With a soft, tender smile, she knelt and held out her arms, gently telling the little ghost, "Come child, it's time. There's nothing to be afraid of."

Reassured by Mother Mary's radiant, joyful smile, the little ghost girl ran into her arms to receive the loving hug awaiting her there. Beaming benevolently down at the little girl, Mother Mary lifted her in her arms as she gracefully stood up. Holding the child securely to her, she turned and walked to the Light. Before she entered, she turned back once again and told me, "Bless you, my child. All is well now, all is well. Go with the Divine and be blessed!"

Then she and the little girl were gone.

I was left standing alone, once again aware of the cemetery and its old graves around me. Beth had already walked back down the hill to the entrance where the caretaker was in the process of locking up for the night.

As I walked down to join them, an old saying ran through my mind that was so applicable to those spirits trapped by their issues in the Ghost Realm: "You can never go home again."

Well, you can! It just depends on which Home you're trying to go to!

THE GANGSTER IN THE GRAY HOUSE

The city of Roswell is an affluent northern suburb of Atlanta, Georgia, located on the northern banks of the Chattahoochee River. It was incorporated in 1854 and named for its founder, Roswell King, a wealthy cotton planter and mill owner.

Although Roswell is now quite a progressive, modern town, it has still managed to keep its small-town charm. Even a lot of the old homes reflect this charm. One glaring exception to this charm, though, is an uninhabited home called the Gray House. In truth, this average-looking building, with its peeling gray paint and exposed, weathered boards, has no official name. If it did, though, it would go by the nickname bestowed upon it by the locals: the Spooky House! Why, you ask? Because, by repute, it's loaded with otherworldly types!

I first became aware of one of these ghosts, or rather *some* of them, when some friends asked me to go with them to investigate the Gray House. They wanted to gather evidence of ghosts by hopefully getting EVPs of the ghosts' voices on their recording equipment and apparitions and orbs on their cameras. Orbs are balls of light that are manifestations of ghostly energy. My friends reasoned that because I'm able to see and talk to ghosts, it would be a good idea to take me along. I was to give them an edge by locating the ghosts.

It was a dark night (of course) when we arrived at the old house. The nondescript, gray, wooden building sat back a ways from the street and down a little hill. As we approached, nothing about it appeared out of the ordinary. It did have a gloomy appearance, but one could attribute this to the twilight setting and the scraggly, overhanging trees around it.

Yet as we drew closer to the house, the energy began to shift. It felt like we had walked through a cold, damp curtain of air. The temperature around the house was drastically lower than that of the surrounding air we'd come through.

I thought, *Oh good, definite evidence of a paranormally active location.* If I had known how haunted the old house really was, I would have been jumping for joy! My friends, on the other hand, were starting to get spooked by the heavy atmosphere around the house. Even though they couldn't see them, they were definitely feeling the energy of the otherworldly beings that inhabited the location.

They were going to get even more spooked when I told them about the man—or rather, the ghost of a man—I saw watching us from an upstairs window. Knowing the reaction I'd get, because of my mischievous sense of humor, I told them to take some photos of that upstairs window. One of the women gave a startled gasp as she looked at what her camera had captured. There, on the screen, was the nebulous figure of the ghostly man! As the group stood there stunned, I continued to watch the ghost as he continued to watch us. It wasn't curiosity I was picking up from him as he stared at us, but anger and malevolence. The heavy, oppressive energy permeating the place was coming from him and whatever had gone on here in the past.

As he continued to stare, there was such an attitude of hatred in his hard gaze I became intrigued as to why. What made him the way he was, and why was he still here?

Just then, a woman in the group complained of feeling nauseous. Someone else said they had suddenly gotten a bad headache. It was obviously time to go, as the energy of the place was getting too uncomfortable for some of the group. Before we could leave though, one of the guys, Todd, asked what was causing the sudden headaches and nausea. "Yeah, what's going on?" they all wanted to know.

I explained, "The male ghost in the window is probably a lower-level ghost. A lower-level ghost, unlike most other ghosts, exists at a much heavier vibrational frequency, just as they did while in the physical. What were their thoughts and actions while in the physical? Were they violent, manipulative, unscrupulous? This heavy, negative energy—accrued during the physical from harmful, negative actions—follows and weighs them down in death, putting them on a lower level in the Ghost Realm. This heavier energy, whether from someone such as a career criminal or a lower-level ghost, can permeate the lighter energy of a human, causing an energetic conflict for the person. This conflict can sometimes cause physical symptoms such as the ones you're experiencing." Seeing looks of concern in the group, I quickly reassured them that the negative effects were usually temporary. Once the human moves out of the area of the source of heavy energy, the effects tend to dissipate.

"Why would we be affected in the first place?" Raymond, another one of the guys, asked.

"Well, we humans are first and foremost spiritual (energetic) beings, so we do get energetically affected and influenced by the positive or negative vibrations of whoever or whatever we're around," I explained as I thought of the old maxim "Be careful who you hang with—they could bring you down!" (Of course, we know they can't bring us down unless we choose, either consciously or unconsciously, to let them! Free will, remember?)

Anyway, after some in the group saw how others were beginning to be affected, they decided they too had had enough of the paranormal for one night. As I turned to leave with them, something made me pause and look back. The malevolent ghost was looking right at me with a concentrated stare, guaranteed to draw my attention! What did he want? Did he even know? At that moment I decided to come back at a later date to check out the ghost and get his story.

***

It was several months later before I managed to get back to the Gray House. I brought along my good friends and fellow psychics Peggy Stancil and Lisalyn Jackson to help with the investigation and to take photographs.

Although the sun shone brightly on the warm, summer day we arrived, the house still had a heavy, gloomy air wrapped around it. As we walked around the house taking photos and getting closer and closer to its energy, Lisalyn, a gifted empath, felt nauseated. It got so bad, she had to leave the premises and wait in the car.

As Peggy and I approached the back side of the house, I noticed a dark crawlspace with its door open, hanging off its hinges. I told Peggy I was being energetically drawn to it, so I wanted to go in and check it out.

Magnanimously I asked Peggy, "Would you like to go in and explore it with me?"

"No way! I'll let you have the whole crawlspace to yourself!" she stated generously.

Hmm, was Peggy spooked by the crawlspace itself or by some strange energy emanating from it? Whatever, in I went without her.

The crawlspace where the three little ghost girls were trapped

I had to bend over to go through the opening. As I entered the crawlspace, I realized how cramped and small it was. The energy of the tiny room felt very heavy and oppressive. The air was so cold and thick, I could see my breath! It felt like I had stepped into a deep freezer.

Peggy snapped a picture as I was stepping in. I saw quick movement and heard a frightened, startled gasp. When I looked closer, there, back in the gloom and shadows, were three little ghost girls. They were huddled together on a bench against the back wall, or rather *sitting in the air* on the spot where the bench used to be.

Peggy, unaware of the little ghost girls, snapped another picture. The bright camera flash startled the little ghosts once again. One cried out and threw her arms up in front of her face. It appeared to be a pitiful attempt to protect herself from attack. I could feel the fear emanating from the little girls as they shrank back against the wall. They couldn't have been more than five or six years old.

I tried to make my movements slow and nonthreatening as I sat down on a dusty old board. It was either that or sit on the dirt floor among the trash, leaves, and rodent litter. I could see and feel my guides and angels gathering around me. They're always with me to guide and protect me, especially when I'm working with spirits. They're the ones who handle the Spirit Realm side of my work while I do the physical. When I'm helping ghosts cross over, I can only go so far because the physical part of me anchors me in the Earth Realm. The angels will take the spirits the rest of the way, making sure they arrive safely at their true Home, the Other Side. They also help protect me from negative paranormal energies and influences. I wouldn't go anywhere without Black Hawk, my main guide, and Archangel Michael!

I'm not the only human that has Divine help available at all times, though. Every spirit that comes to live temporarily in the Earth Realm in a physical body has their own personal team of Divine helpers, their guides and angels. They're always with us. We just forget about them sometimes, but they never do us!

The dark energy in this old house and its crawlspace made it one of those times I was glad for this Divine aid.

So, knowing that I was not alone, ghosts included, I began to calmly communicate with the fearful little ghost girls. Recognizing their need to get used to my presence, I sat there and sent them loving energy. I could see the angels starting to gather around them to comfort and calm their fears. They definitely needed it. They had been so traumatized by someone or something while alive that even in death they were literally still shaking with fear.

As time passed and I made no move to harm them, I could feel their fear starting to abate. Finally, the little ghost girl in the middle began to fidget. She was a little brunette with curly hair and bangs. Knowing her childish curiosity was getting the better of her, I gave her a big smile.

"Who are you?" she asked, gathering her courage.

"My name is Boo," I said with a grin.

Giggling in that open, innocent way only the young at heart have, she exclaimed, "That's a funny name! I like it!"

Hmm, I thought, *a contrary view to that of a lot of the adults I've met.*

Looking back at the little girl and her companions in mutual amusement, I asked her, "What is your name?"

"I'm Emily!" she proudly declared. Then, being quite the little leader, she took it upon herself to introduce the other little ghost girls. "This here's Ruthie Ann and Mae."

Ruthie Ann appeared to be a shy little girl with sandy-brown hair and freckles. She stared back at me with big, brown eyes. Mae was a blond, blue-eyed child who would have grown into a stunningly beautiful woman if her life hadn't been cut short. She started to speak, but then ebullient Emily broke in with, "Guess how old I am!"

Knowing it would tickle her to think she looked much older, I told her, "Why, you must be nine years old!"

At this obvious ripper on my part, all three little girls burst out giggling in unabashed merriment. When the laughter died down, Emily replied, "I'm only six years old, but I'll be seven in June. Mama said I could have a party!"

At the little ghost girl's excitement, a sadness came over me. I teared up as I realized that for the little ghost girl, there would be no more birthdays for her to celebrate. My thoughts now taking a more somber tact, I wondered what had caused the three little ghosts to be trapped in this dank, dark crawlspace. Knowing Ruthie Ann was still too shy to answer, I asked Mae how they got here.

"The bad men brung us!" she said tearfully.

At her words, Ruthie Ann withdrew even more into herself. Emily and Mae also now fell silent, glancing around fearfully. Who or what were they watching out for? Their great fear was palpable in the air around us.

Looking at Emily, I gently asked, "What happened to you and Mae and Ruthie Ann? How come you are here?"

"The bad men hurt us and hurt us and hurt us!" she exclaimed in distress. She started crying uncontrollably. I wanted to hug her but couldn't because of the different energetic forms we inhabited. So instead, I did the next best thing. I sent her and the others loving energy, telling them that they were loved and had nothing to fear. The angels would protect their spirits from any harm. Even now, the loving energy of the angels was starting to calm the three little ghost girls.

When they had calmed down enough, I tried once again to get their stories. "Are you aware you have died?" I asked quietly.

"Yes," they answered softly.

"Why are you still here if you know you're no longer alive in the physical?"

"We don't know where to go, and the mean man won't let us out!"

"What mean man? How did you die?" Yet once again, all the three little ghosts could tell me was that the mean men had hurt them.

I realized that they didn't have the vocabulary at their young ages to tell me what befell them. Because of their youth, when death overtook them they had no references from older life experiences to draw from. Once again they fell silent, mutely watching me from tear-filled eyes. I too became silent as I listened to my guides and angels fill me in on the past happenings that had taken place in this dark house. Their words filled me with dread and horror over what the three little girls had been forced to endure during their short lives.

Boo working with the ghosts in the crawlspace

My guides and angels told me that the male ghost in the upstairs window had been called John when he was in the earthly realm. He had been born around the turn of the twentieth century, yet the main part of his life story occurred from the early 1920s up to the late 1940s.

He had been the son of a prominent local family. His family had had wealth and position. Despite this, his had not been a happy childhood. His father had been a miserable, controlling man. He had been very hard on John, even when he was a young child.

Physical and verbal abuse were meted out to the boy at the slightest infraction. Little John was constantly ridiculed in front of others for being a "weakling" and "not worth the food it took to feed him." It was also nothing for John to be mercilessly beaten by the older man. John's father didn't spare his mother from this abuse, either. He watched many times as his mother was battered and bruised by her husband when he was in one of his drunken rages.

Someone once dared to ask him why he was so hard on John when he seemed to be a good lad. John's father had coldly replied, "I'm trying to toughen him up, make a man of him!"

When John left boyhood, he rebelled and fell in with the local criminal elements operating in the area. These criminals were involved in all types of vice, such as murder, extortion, illegal alcohol, drugs, gambling, and prostitution. The most reprehensible activity the gang benefited from was child prostitution.

John himself was a pedophile. He ran this part of the business for the gang. Through his family's connections with some of the local law officers, he could operate above the law. It was understood that as long as the gang kept a low profile in the community, they could, and did, operate with impunity.

The Gray House was one of John's properties. It served as a holding location during the transport of the children who were being forced into prostitution. They were kept locked in the dark crawlspaces under the house. The girls used by the gang ranged in age from four and five years old up to thirteen and fourteen. As the debauched patrons of the house were fond of saying, "John always has the freshest meat on the street!" Every now and then a young boy was brought through for the customers with different perversions.

The children exploited were orphans, or had been bought or stolen from impoverished families. The desperate, gullible family had been assured that their child was going to a better life. They had no idea how far from the truth this claim was.

The young victims were beaten to keep them in line and drugged to keep them quiet. After being sexually abused at the house for days or weeks, they would then be moved to new locations where further horrible abuse took place. When they had been used up, they were discarded like trash wherever they happened to be.

John and his gang were smart enough not to foul their own nest. The children were brought from communities and rural areas much farther away. This was how the gang kept the good citizens of Roswell ignorant of the true nature of the activities taking place at the Gray House. Oh, sometimes strange, unexplained noises and screams were heard coming from the house at night by someone strolling by. Usually the passersby knew better than to seek an explanation, though. John was known to be a very mean man to mess with. Most of the time the odd sounds were attributed to the hard partying of the rough friends John was wont to hang with. Maybe John and his friends and the "ladies" were just getting a little rowdy. The law never seemed concerned. Maybe it was best to stay out of someone else's business and look the other way, right?

Whatever the case, the criminal enterprises of the gang were why and how the three little girls, or rather their ghosts, came to be trapped in this dank, dark crawlspace.

One of the little girls, Emily, had been killed and buried on the premises. One of the customers had gotten rough with her one night and broken her neck. Ah well, no great loss to the gang. To them she was expendable, disposable, and easily replaced.

Ruthie Ann and Mae had died at another gang location close by and had gravitated back to the crawlspace, drawn by Emily's energy. They had no idea as to where else to go. After they had arrived back here in spirit, the terrifying energy of the house and the ghost of John kept them chained to it. They still feared him as much in death as they had in life.

That is why, when Peggy's camera flash went off, they shrank back in fear. They didn't recognize it for the harmless thing it was. Because they had been imprisoned in the dark crawlspaces for days and weeks, light signaled pain. To them, when the door opened and light was let in, it always meant they were about to be dragged out to the horrible abuse and mistreatment awaiting them.

Now I understood why they were too petrified to move off the bench. With this in mind, I once again started talking to the three little ghosts in a loving, reassuring tone. As I was telling them about the angels that were there to help them, their eyes suddenly darted to something behind me.

"He's here!" little Mae whispered fearfully to the others. It was as though she felt that if she were quiet enough, whatever was behind me wouldn't notice her. The energy and temperature in the crawlspace became much more oppressive and cold. Without turning around, I knew John, the gangster ghost, was coming through the wall, approaching me from behind.

He was so angry and incensed over my presence and interference, I could hear him growling at me as he came closer. With his proximity the cold around me intensified. The little ghost girls were staring at him from round, fearful eyes, frozen by his presence.

"Who are you?" he growled. "What do you want?"

"I've come to help you and the other ghosts trapped in this house!" I stated firmly.

There are times to be soft when working with troubled spirits, but then there are times to exhibit a tough, no-nonsense exterior. This obviously was going to be one of those times.

"We want no help. YOU don't belong here!" the gangster ghost angrily spat.

"Neither do you nor the other ghosts who are here," I shot back. "And it's their choice if they want help or not, not yours!"

Turning my attention back to the ghosts of Emily, Ruthie Ann, and Mae, I could hear him still muttering ominously behind me as I now ignored him. Their fearful, frozen faces clearly showed the great terror that bound the little ghost girls to the gangster. I told them that they now had nothing to fear from him. "He has no more power to hurt you."

Even as I spoke, the angels were moving to protectively surround the children. Because of this, despite the terrifying energy that had come in with John, the energy around the little ghost girls started to become lighter and lighter. They were now paying more attention to the bright, beautiful beings around them than they were to the dark ghost.

Their faces began to reflect the glow of joy and love that radiated from the angelic beings. The time for them to go Home was rapidly approaching. Pointing to the right, I asked them, "Do you see the golden Light?"

"Yes!" they squealed excitedly as they looked at the glowing Light and its multicolored sparkles. All three jumped up and down and laughed in unfettered joy.

The energy of unconditional love radiating from the beautiful, golden Light of the Divine had begun to fill the once-gloomy crawlspace. The little ghost girls could now feel this energy of complete love as they absorbed it into their beings. There was no more fear and sorrow. Hope and joy had erased them.

They were now ready to accompany the angels into the Light. Excitement and joy shone on their faces as the angels gathered around them, and three of the great angels stepped forward and slowly knelt down in front of the little girls. Gently picking up each little girl, Emily, Ruthie Ann, and Mae now found themselves held securely in the loving arms of the powerful beings. The angel holding Emily even smiled mischievously as he turned his hair blue for her, which of course added to the merriment of the precocious little girl. Her blue-haired angel proved once again how right the adage "What better companion for a child than an angel!" is.

Turning once again toward the Light, the group walked over to it. Before entering, the little ghost girls had their angels stop and turn back toward us. Grinning, they gleefully hollered, "Bye Boo! Bye Boo!" Then, looking at John, they told him, "We love you." It was their way of trying to tell John they forgave him for what he had done to them.

Turning back to the Light, the group stepped in. As they did, Emily playfully ruffled her angel's blue hair with her small hand, exclaiming, "Why is your hair blue? My hair is brown. Mama said I better let her brush . . ." and then they were gone!

The angels told me they made it safely Home to the Other Side where loved ones were waiting for them.

Now for the gangster. He had approached closer and was standing behind my right shoulder. He was hesitant to come any closer because of my two big guardian angels, Orion and Aegius. They were standing protectively on either side of me, as they always do when I'm working with spirits.

There was now an air of confusion around the gangster ghost. His anger had cooled down considerably. After watching the little ghost girls cross over to the Other Side, the energy radiating off him didn't feel so dark and forbidding. John had started to feel the power of peace that results from forgiving ourselves and others.

I told him it was okay for him to come closer. Orion and Aegius stepped aside to allow this. I now got my first good look at John, the gangster ghost, as he stepped in front of me. He was a man of average height, about five foot ten and heavily built. His brown hair was thin and unkempt, as were his clothes. There was an unhealthy pallor about his skin that had resulted from the hard drinking and debauchery he had indulged in while alive.

"Why are you still here after all these years instead of going into the Light? Don't you know you've died?"

"Yes, of course I know I'm dead!" he snapped. "But here in this house I'm still powerful and in control and respected! I don't want to give that up."

It was true. His evil-feeling energy still scared people, even if it now came from his ghost instead of the living man. It was obvious that even in death, as when alive, he still craved the respect and power denied him in his youth. He had tried so hard and in vain to win his father's respect and love when young. But after having failed to do this, he had given up trying. As time passed and he grew older and harder, he hadn't cared any more where this respect and power came from, or what he had to do to get it, as long as he got it. Was he ready to give up this false power now?

I had to find out before I left the crawlspace.

"Do you want to go into the Light, to cross over?" I asked.

"I'm not sure," he cautiously replied.

Now, when doing a clearing, I can force a stuck spirit to move on to other physical locations. But I can't, and would not try to, force a ghost to go into the Light. That would be disrespectful. This is because all spirits have the Divinely given right of free will to decide for themselves.

Yet I could still try to help John decide to cross over by helping him find clarity with the issue that was trapping him. "What is holding you in the Ghost Realm, John?"

"The fear I have of my father is too great. I can't forgive him either for his cruelty to me as a boy. I don't want to face him!" he emphatically stated.

As if John's words had called to him (which in reality they had), the air in the crawlspace shifted as John's father materialized in front of us, accompanied by angels. John stepped back in alarm at his father's sudden appearance. Gone was the bravado of the gangster. He was once again that shy, powerless little boy. But this father was different than the one he had known in life. Instead of cruelty and disgust on his face, there were tears. He held out his arms, beckoning his son to him.

John at first resisted giving in to the yearning for his father's love as memories of the cruelties inflicted on him flooded his being. Then, even though fearing that it was too good to be true, John slowly and fearfully approached his father. His father met him halfway and pulled John into his arms. As he hugged John in a tight embrace, he leaned close and whispered something in his ear. The only word I overheard was "love," but whatever the rest was, it caused John's face to light up with joy.

His father now coaxed John to follow him into the Light. For some reason, though, John was still hesitant about crossing over. Even though he and his father had reconciled in love, something else still didn't feel right with John. What was it?

Nonetheless, he followed his father to the Light, intending to cross with him. His father and the angels stepped into it and disappeared. John started to step in, but just at the last moment he hesitated then backed away. The portal of Light closed. John moaned as he realized that his decision had locked him out of the door to peace, the door that would have led to the healing power of understanding and peace and love found on the Other Side. He broke down in tears of despair.

What was going on?

He had accepted forgiveness for himself from the little girls. He had in turn forgiven himself, and his father, for their cruelties and misdeeds while alive. So what was still holding John trapped in the Ghost Realm?

At the moment the ghost was too upset for me to talk to him. It was time to go once again to my guides and angels. "What does the ghost gangster need to help him cross over?" I asked.

Black Hawk, my main guide, filled me in on the rest of John's story. "There's someone that he doesn't want to leave behind. It's the ghost of his girlfriend in life. She loved him unconditionally, but because he was unable to love himself, which would have enabled him to know that he was worthy of such love, he didn't appreciate her true worth. He mistreated her horribly.

"When they first got together she had been a fine, upstanding young woman. She believed that she could help John discover the better part of himself. Instead, because of her blind love for him, he corrupted her. He pimped her out to other men. Over time she spiraled down into a world of alcohol, drugs, and prostitution.

"Late one night, she died in the house from an overdose of drugs and alcohol. Because of the drugs, she died in an emotionally and mentally confused state. Therefore, when her spirit left its physical body at the time of death, she was still in this confused state. The ghost thought she had regained consciousness like she had done so many times before after passing out. She was, in fact, dead, and had left her physical body for good.

"The young woman had always wanted to get her life straightened out, dreaming of how it would be when this happened. John would love her and marry her. They would have children. But she was never able to turn her life around, and then, with her death, it was too late. She has remained trapped ever since because of her inability to comprehend and accept her abrupt passage."

Turning back to John, I asked him if he had been trying to help her understand her true state of existence, death.

"Yes," he replied, "I've been going to her to try to help her accept her death. She becomes terrified whenever I get near her, though. She knows I'm dead because she was with me when I died after getting shot. She believes she's still alive, though. Because of this, she believes I'm trying to haunt her. When I approach her she always screams and yells at me, 'Go away, leave me alone!' "

(This reaction can happen when a spirit tries to rescue another spirit who's in denial over their own death. The spirit who's being rescued knows the other spirit is dead in the physical. They "know" that they themselves are "alive." So, because of their confusion over their passing, they fear they're being haunted by the dead person. This confusion over their true state of existence also increases the difficulty of helping them cross over.)

"I don't know how to help her!" John said with a heavy sigh of despair.

I realized that he really loved his girlfriend. The problem was he hadn't known this until it was too late. She had been unable to trust him in life, and so was now unable to trust him in death. *What a quandary for the pair,* I sadly thought. *Each one wanting to help the other from love but still unable to.*

Because of John's guilt over how he had abused her during their long relationship while alive, he now refused to move on without her in death. She would not go with him because of her confused belief that she was still alive and so still had the chance to turn her life around.

As I pondered the ghosts' dilemma, Peggy came to the door and drew my attention to the failing light outside. Within a short time it would be dark outside and even darker in this dank, cold crawlspace. I didn't have a flashlight and so didn't relish the thought of groping my way out of this dark, oppressive space.

It was time to go and rejoin the world of the physically alive.

I asked John one last time if he wanted to go into the Light. "Not without her!" he stated tearfully. I then promised him that I would return later to see if she was ready. The only consolation I could leave him with in his desolation was that the angels were even now working with her, and that I would do my best to help them when I returned. I then left the crawlspace, leaving behind a no-longer-nasty gangster but a forlorn John.

***

I didn't get a chance to return to the Gray House until several months later. Dusk was approaching by the time I arrived after being trapped in one of Atlanta's infamous traffic jams. Once again Lisalyn came with me, but this time with a sense of trepidation. The first time she had come she was overcome by nausea from being in the oppressive, heavy energy of the place and its ghostly inhabitants. The nausea had been so bad, she had had to leave the premises and sit in the car. This time, much to our relief, she experienced no nausea. In fact, as she walked around the house and its grounds, she was amazed at how different the energy felt between our first visit and now. For, even though the heaviness was not totally gone, the air felt much lighter and brighter.

As we approached the house, the ghost of the gangster peered out at us from his upstairs window. His gaze conveyed hope this time instead of anger. I thought, *Someone's been busy!* The angels had been using the energy of their Divine love on the situation.

Once again, we headed for the dirty crawlspace. In the spirit of generosity, I offered to share it with Lisalyn. After peering into the dark, dank place she demurred, saying, "I'll sit on the bench over here and meditate for a while. Holler if you need me!"

Leaving her ensconced on her bench, I turned to the crawlspace and, bending over once again, entered. I had barely sat on my dirty board when the ghost of an elderly white woman materialized beside me. Her faded-gray hair was done up in a bun, but the thin strands of hair straggling around her wrinkled face made it look unkempt. The ill-fitting, old dress she wore made her thin frame look even bonier. A quiet and sorrowful energy emanated off her, and there was an air of subservience about her. The deep lines etching her old face were proof of a life hard lived.

"Who are you?" I asked.

"I was John's house servant."

There was no pride in her voice when she said this, only deep shame and regret. The ghost went on to tell me that her younger years had been used up and destroyed by a life of alcohol and prostitution. When her usefulness as a prostitute came to an end, she had been made the unofficial housekeeper of this dreadful house.

There was so much guilt and shame and regret around the old ghost woman, she refused to look at me. "I knew of the ghastly activities going on in this house," she said, "but what could I do? I had no power. Can you help me? I don't know where to go and I don't want to stay here any longer."

I was about to tell her about the Other Side when the ghost of John materialized in front of me accompanied by a female ghost in her thirties. I also sensed that the ghost of a large black man was standing behind me, patiently waiting for something. I asked him to step in front of me, which he did. He looked at me with a hopeful expression written on his gentle face. There was a scar running across his left cheek and down his chin. A life hard lived, but not by choice. Faded, blue overalls hung off his broad frame and he wore no shirt underneath them. His work boots were old and run down at the heels.

"Who are you?" I asked.

"I was the handyman and cleaning man of the house." He fell silent as a tear trickled down his dusty face. Once again, as with the ghost of the old woman, I sensed that this silence came more from shame than shyness.

My angels filled me in on the ghost's previous physical life. They said that the ghost, when alive, had been accused of a crime as a young man. It was not a serious crime and he had been innocent. But because of the times, there had been no defense and no justice for the young black man. He had been headed for a prison work camp when the gang "rescued" him. They brought him back to this area and he had lived in fear of exposure ever since. He had been used by them to clean up after nasty pieces of gang business, such as murder and extortion. He would get rid of the evidence and dispose of the bodies.

"What do you want?" I gently asked him.

"I want to leave here. I want to be free," he stated.

"Then you will be!" I answered with firm reassurance. I could say this with confidence because even now the angels were assembling all around us, ready to assist in working with these confused, fearful souls.

I now turned back to John, who had been patiently waiting during my exchange with the ghost of the big handyman. Pointing to the ghost of the dark-haired young woman, I asked, "Is this the woman you refuse to leave behind?"

"Yes, she was my woman in life. She loved me then but hates me now." A sigh of deep sadness tinged his voice.

He hadn't needed to tell me this, as the state of their relationship was clear. When working with multiple spirits, you can deduce what the energy and quality of their relationship was while alive by where they stand in proximity to each other in death. The young woman who had accompanied John to the crawlspace was standing far apart from him, watching him guardedly. I could see that at one time she had been a beautiful creature with rich, chestnut-colored hair. Over time, though, her features had become lined and coarse, and the beautiful hair matted and streaked with gray as her hard life overcame her. Where once her figure had been stunning and full, the drugs, alcohol, and prostitution had destroyed it to where it was now: emaciated and thin.

As I continued to observe her, she warily watched me and John. I could see the air of confusion increasing around her as she studied both of us. She could not help but notice the obvious difference in our energies. Mine was the denser energy of the Earth Realm, and his was the lighter energy of the Spirit Realm. I could hear her confused wondering, *Where do I belong? John's dead but I'm not—or am I? How could this be? I'm awake now, not dead!*

On and on her confused thoughts ran. This confusion originated from a loss of memory of her death. She would have to remember her death and accept it before she would be able to grant herself freedom from the realm of ghosts. She was so confused, though. Was I going to be able to help her?

Suddenly nausea overtook my physical body, and I felt like I was choking and gagging. What was going on? I knew these sensations didn't belong to me. I was feeling them secondhand through the ability of clairsentience. This is the psychic ability that enables someone to pick up on and feel the emotions and/or physical sensations being experienced by another. Who was I picking up the choking sensations from? It felt like I was about to be strangled to death!

Looking at the ghost of the young woman, I realized the answer was standing right in front of me. For there, on the ghost woman's face, neck, and in her hair, was the dried residue of brown vomit. Everything became clear to me. But was it clear to the confused ghost herself? To help her find this clarity, I asked her, "What was the last thing you remember before you passed out?"

A look of surprise at my knowing this crossed her drawn, pale face. "I'd been drinking all day," she answered. "That afternoon I found some morphine lying around, so I took that. The next thing I know I'm rolling around on the floor—my stomach was cramping that bad! I threw up. I felt so sick I thought I was going to die! I passed out, but thank God I woke up later."

The ghost of the young woman paused for a moment in her narrative. Now was my chance!

"Oh, but you didn't wake up, at least not in the realm of the physically alive," I told her. "Your 'waking up,' as you call it, was your spirit stepping out of its now-deceased body."

A look of stubborn disbelief and shock crossed her face. In a voice filled with panic, she exclaimed, "But how can this be? I'm awake, awake, awake, I tell you, alive!"

"Yes, you're awake and alive, but not alive in the same realm as I am, that of the earthly, physical one. As you lost consciousness, you choked to death on your own vomit. At that moment you died in the physical!"

At my words, startled confusion spread across the ghost's face. Dazed, she repeated my own words to herself. "I choked to death on my own vomit. I choked to death on my own vomit." Then the truth hit her hard. "I choked to death on my own vomit!" she exclaimed in horror. With this realization, the young woman fell apart. She started crying. Over and over the ghost sobbed in anguish, "Oh, my God, my God, oh what have I done with my life? My God, what have I done?"

There was so much grief and remorse and self-loathing in her voice, I couldn't help but feel great compassion and sorrow for her emotional suffering. She doubled over, sobbing with despair and regret. John approached her to comfort her, but she would have none of it. Throwing her arm out toward him with palm facing out, she screamed, "Get away from me, you monster!" John shrank back from her with a look of bleak despair.

Meanwhile, the angels were arriving in the crawlspace in increasing numbers, gathering around John, his girlfriend, the old housekeeper, and the handyman. I was relieved to see the angels because the latter two ghosts looked frightened and ready to bolt at the sight of the younger, female ghost's emotional outburst.

Now, due to the effect of the angels' energy of unconditional love bathing the group, they started to calm down. It was even affecting John's girlfriend, for she was no longer sobbing. It was becoming obvious that the group of ghosts was beginning to feel the perfect peace that is found in the perfect love of the Divine, as represented by these Divine angelic beings.

Once again, John approached his girlfriend and took her hand. At first she pulled back and looked at him in residual anger. *Oh no,* I thought, *she's going to reject him again!* But no, some part of his genuine love for her must have touched her being, for she suddenly smiled at him, her now-glowing face saying it all. "I love you and forgive you, John," she said. "Thank you for waiting for me."

United now in love as they had never been in life, the two ghost lovers turned back to me. The other two ghosts now joined them.

"What now?" the old housekeeper timidly asked.

I talked to the group of ghosts, telling them how much they were loved by the Divine. I told them that the healing, peace, and joy that had eluded them in life were still theirs to claim because of their Divine birthright. They could still have them, and it was never too late.

"Where can we find this perfect love and joy?" the ghost of John's girlfriend asked.

"The angels will take you to it. They'll escort you to the Other Side where this Divine love awaits all spirits who desire it."

I now saw the golden Light, the portal to the Other Side, opening up to the group of ghosts. I pointed to it. "There's the entrance to the Other Side. All you have to do is follow the angels into the Light."

The angels, meanwhile, had been moving among the group of ghosts, readying them for the journey Home. John the ex-gangster and his girlfriend, as well as the other two ghosts, now turned toward the Light. No longer lost but now found, they walked with newfound hope and understanding toward it, accompanied by their angels.

The young woman gasped, "Mama!" There, standing at the entrance to the Light, was her mother. There were tears of joy streaming down her face.

"I've been waiting ever so long for you, honey!" she told her daughter. Her baby was finally coming Home!

There were also other loved ones waiting to greet each one of the group of rescued spirits. Amid much joyful laughter and many hugs, the group of ghosts and their loved ones and angels walked into the Light. It closed and I was left behind. I could see no more.

One of the angels had stayed behind to escort me out of the now-dark crawlspace. The energy around me felt lighter and brighter. As I stepped out of the crawlspace and into the velvety night, I could see the stars twinkling brightly above me, shining representations of the eternal, Universal Love of the Divine. Despite the Dark, all would be well.

THE GUARDIANS OF GOST CAVE

I have watched my good friend David Dean as he walked across a barren field, stop, drop to his knees, and start digging. From a foot down, up would come an ancient spearhead held in his hand! How did he do it?

Or what about the time he went into a wooded area and said, "Go twenty feet in that direction, dig down, and you'll uncover evidence of an ancient American Indian site." The dig happens, uncovering an ancient fireplace. This, after all the experts said there was nothing of great archaeological value there.

Where does this uncanny ability of David's to intuitively discover important American Indian sites and artifacts come from?

Maybe looking at the man will explain it. David is a historian, archaeologist, paleontologist, geologist, and mineralogist, and he is proficient in American Indian studies of all different tribes and cultures. What's so amazing about these talents is that they're all rolled up into one modest man. He is one of the most brilliant individuals I have ever met in my long life. And trust me, I'm not the type to bestow this term lightly.

Although he would be considered a layperson by most so-called experts, he is the first person they contact when they need answers and can't find them anywhere else. In fact, many a college student owes the success of their masters and doctorate theses to David's generosity in sharing the vast knowledge he's accumulated over the years from studying his varied interests.

There's not a shred of ego about the man, though. He is so unassuming, in fact, that when you first meet him, you have no inkling of this vast storeroom of knowledge contained in his being. It's only when you get to know David, as I have been privileged to, that you realize the storeroom holds not only information about earthly matters, but also great cosmic knowledge as well. I suspect that it's this cosmic knowledge, along with some deep connection he has with Mother Earth and her former ancient inhabitants, that enables him to walk into the woods and discover something historically important from supposedly nothing.

Even David himself is not sure how he's able to do certain things. When questioned, he will tell you that he's had these abilities since he was a boy. By the time he was a grown man, all he had to do was hone them to a finely tuned edge. David's talents and abilities have kept him occupied. What with his writing (did I forget to mention he's a published author?), working on archaeological digs, speaking engagements, research, and communicating with colleagues in his various fields of interest, David is a very busy man.

That's why, when a month or two went by and there was no word from him, I didn't think anything about it. As his birthday rolled around, though, I wondered why I hadn't heard from him. I left a message when I called David for his birthday and couldn't get him. I had a feeling something big was up (you know me, not wanting to be left out of any adventures, big or small!).

When he called me later, I asked him where he'd been. "In a cave," he replied.

I laughed, thinking he was kidding me. After all, we do call each other "outgoing hermits" because of our penchants for privacy despite our people-oriented careers.

"No really, I've been in a cave. No cell reception!" David explained. He then went on to tell me about Gost Cave.

Although American Indians had known about Gost Cave for thousands of years, and so had the white settlers who came later, no one had thought to explore it. David was the first to realize the potential archaeological importance of the cave. What made this cave so unique was that, on one of the inside walls, he had discovered two sculptures carved on the dolomite surface.

One sculpture was that of a human head and face. The other sculpture was of a jaguar head, complete with the whiskers. They had been placed side by side as if to signify a partnership of some kind.

When David had contacted one of the foremost cave-art experts in the country about the two carvings, the man, after studying the photos David had sent, had trouble controlling his excitement. "Nothing like this cave art has ever been found before in this country!" he exclaimed.

Aside from finding the two mysterious sculptures, David (who's extremely sensitive to any other energies around him) had also picked up some strange, powerful energy emanating throughout the cave—energy he knew was not coming from the group of excited, enthusiastic, young Boy Scouts he had agreed to accompany on their spelunking expedition that day.

Knowing that I would understand because of my own experiences with the supernatural, he told me, "Boo, as I walked through the cave, the hair on the back of my neck stood up!"

Now intrigued by his first experience with Gost Cave, David had returned about a month later by himself to explore the cave further. Unlike most caves he had explored, there was no historical human trash such as pot shards, discarded tools, flint chips, or charcoal from long-ago fires to give mute evidence of human usage throughout the centuries. Had it been a sacred place kept clean because of its holiness? There was not even any modern trash in the cave. Could this dearth of modern trash be silent testament to the possibility that the cave's reputation for being haunted had kept most would-be interlopers out?

As early as the late 1600s, when the first whites arrived in the area for the purpose of trading with the Cherokee, the cave was reputed to be haunted, hence these early settlers giving the cave the name "Hainted" or "Gost" Cave. Probably because of the illiteracy of these early traders and settlers, they spelled the cave's name "Gost" instead of the more correct spelling, "Ghost." Although no one knows for sure who named it, one thing is known for certain: the name Gost is fitting for this cave.

In fact, the few people who dared to go into the cave throughout the centuries came out with tales of, as they put it, "hearing the walls talk!" Others told of hearing what sounded like deep male voices around them, and glimpsing in the dim glow cast by their lanterns dark shadow figures flitting throughout the stone rooms. Some people have even felt presences around them that they can't see, and things brushing by them in the dark.

Tom, a boyhood friend of David's, told him that the grandfather of one of his friends warned him not to go into Gost Cave because it was haunted. Even the American Indians in the area had avoided the cave throughout the centuries. Their reason for avoiding the cave didn't come from fear, though, so much as the belief that the cave, and the mountain it's located in, is a sacred place protected by powerful spirit beings.

The other mountains in this area were also held to be sacred. These mountains are where the ancient ones lived before the more modern tribes, such as the Cherokee, came into existence. Are the Cherokee modern descendants of these ancient people? In fact, there's evidence that the name Cherokee was derived from a word used by the Delaware, Choctaw, and Iroquois that translates as "people of the cave" or "cave people."

No one knows what happened to these ancient people, but the powerful energy they left behind still resonates throughout this part of the Great Smoky and Blue Ridge Mountains to this day.

Even the mountains themselves, because of their geological makeup, have one of the highest concentrations of electromagnetic energy found anywhere on earth. Could this intense geological energy be what drew these ancient people to this area in the first place? Their wise ones and shamans must have realized that this powerful earth energy would serve to amplify their own energy to unprecedented high levels.

This powerful earth energy they tapped into, connected with, was created by the high number of strong vortexes and ley lines found throughout the area. A vortex is an area of energy created by a spiraling motion of air, water, or spiritual energy around a center of rotation. Ley lines are lines of energy found running around the earth in patterns forming grids. Ley lines form what could be called the nervous system of earth.

Another source of earth energy that the ancients could utilize was the energy found in Gost Cave itself and other such locations throughout the region. This amped-up earth energy in Gost Cave comes from the large deposits of calcite found there. Calcite is similar to quartz in that, under conditions of an extreme amount of pressure on them, they both release a type of electricity. This piezoelectric energy radiates into the surrounding environment, charging up whatever it meets.

But it was not only this naturally occurring earth energy that David felt while digging through the cave-floor dirt looking for artifacts for his research. He told me, "Boo, while I was working in the cave I felt a large presence standing off to my side, watching me as I moved around. Then, on the way home, I became aware that there was something in the car with me. I couldn't see it, but it was there nonetheless. After I got home and settled in, it was still with me in my apartment. Whatever it was stayed with me for over a month, watching me. One day I woke up and it was gone. It felt like I had passed a test of some kind."

All this intriguing information was running through my mind as I drove to Tennessee to meet David one weekend. Knowing my interest in anything mysterious and/or otherworldly, he had invited me to come check out Gost Cave.

My friend Beth came along, as she can never pass up an opportunity to check out an area she's never been to before. I think the real reason was that she was worried she might miss out on an adventure of some kind. (Adventures, or sometimes misadventures, do seem to crop up whenever I'm around!) Trust me, it did turn out to be quite an adventure!

The cave is on private land and as such is off limits to most people. For that reason, I agreed with David not to tell the exact location. He had been working with the landowner, who had given him permission to explore it archaeologically.

Gost Cave rests on the side of a steep mountain slope about a half mile high. The day before we arrived, it had rained steadily. The soaked ground hadn't had a chance to dry out by the time we started up the steep slope the next morning. We literally had to dig our shoes into the mud to get traction.

Now there's no need to bore you by telling you over and over how many times we slipped and fell in the mud. I'm sure, like me, you abhor redundancy! So, after the first few times of falling in the mud, I quit worrying about the increasing accumulation of the gooey, earthy stuff caking my clothes. Why worry over something I no longer had any control over, right? There was a positive aspect to wearing an accumulation of mud too. It provided protective padding for my bony butt when I fell on it.

David, to my and Beth's chagrin, didn't fall once. Maybe his balancing skills derived from the fact that he had been raised in these mountains. He had spent his boyhood exploring and roaming up and down their steep slopes. He was a most patient guide to us, though, realizing that in the city you don't usually have to traverse such steep, muddy, treacherous terrain.

When we finally made it up the mountain, David told us that we had each gained five inches. I puffed up with pride, thinking he was complimenting us on the character it took, our courageous perseverance, to get up the muddy, steep slope. With his next words, though, he clarified what he had meant, effectively popping the balloon of my swelled ego.

"Yep, there's nothing like a few inches of good, red mud stuck on the bottom of your shoes to give you an instant growth spurt!"

We couldn't help but laugh, for diminutive Beth indeed looked taller now.

As we stepped up to the cave, the first thing I noticed was not the cave itself but the magnificent tree standing to the left above it. It was so huge, it had to be the great-great-grandmother of all the trees of its kind in the area. It measured about eighteen feet around. It was reputed to be well over a hundred years old. I could feel the energy coming off of it from ten feet away. Having a great fondness for trees and their powerful, benign energy, I couldn't resist walking up to give it a hug. I nestled down among its huge roots and trunk folds. Not being able to get my puny arms around its massive trunk, I spread them as wide as I could and hugged, plastering my cheek up against the tree's rough bark. Thus connected, I became aware of an energetic humming and pulsing emanating from the huge tree. It flowed in a continuous stream into my left hand and arm, through my body, and out my right arm and hand, back into the tree. My body was acting like a conductor of energy. My energy was blending and melding with the energy field, the life force, of this massive being.

I thought, *We have become one, if only for a short time.*

Then a feeling of great joy came over me at the realization that there'd be no real separation between the tree and myself when I moved on. No true separation, because we shared the same Universal energy, and always had. The same Divine Life Force that flowed through the tree also flowed through me and all other living beings! Indeed, we're all interconnected and One.

Thanking the great tree for this reminder, and for sharing her powerful life force with me, I disengaged myself from her and proceeded to the mouth of the cave. There, David had fastened a strong rope to a tree outside the cave and dropped it down into the entranceway. It was about an eight- to ten-foot drop down to enter the cave, and the rain had definitely not missed the steep entry slope. It looked quite slippery from top to bottom, and then some!

Holding the rope, David went down it with his usual, steady, mountain-man élan. I went down next, praying all the while that Beth wouldn't jump the gun and start down before I could get out of her way. Unfortunately, I hadn't progressed more than a foot or two down the muddy slope when my feet shot out from under me, landing me flat on my belly.

The bad news was that I was once again covered from head to toe in fresh, wet mud. The good news? I had discovered an easier method to get into the cave than rappelling down the rope. You guessed it, I decided to use the gravity-and-mud technique to descend into the cave. (Okay, okay, I really didn't have a choice, as I couldn't regain my footing on the muddy slope.)

So, sliding down the slope, I arrived unceremoniously onto the cave floor where David was standing. I could see that, unlike me, he was still in pristine condition from his descent. He was trying to keep from laughing but gave up the effort when Beth, through no decision of her own, arrived using the same mud-sliding method as me.

I couldn't help but laugh with David because Beth is very fastidious about her appearance. There's never a hair out of place, so to speak. This time, though, not only was her hair not in place, the strands of hair were sticking up covered in mud. Even Beth couldn't help but laugh at our appearance. (What are good friends for but to help you laugh at yourself?)

Gathering ourselves off the floor, David led us into Gost Cave. We came to a part of the cave David called the gateway area. It was a narrow tunnel that we had to walk sideways through in order to enter the main chamber where the carvings were.

*David Dean squeezing through
the narrow passage into Gost Cave*

The gateway tunnel of Gost Cave appeared to be similar in form and function to the gateway tunnels built by the ancient Egyptians in their tombs and pyramids. These tunnels served to provide a gate of some type, allowing limited access to the main chamber.

Gost Cave's tunnel twisted and turned, and in some places it was so narrow, we were forced to not only turn sideways but to squeeze through. Could this tunnel, with its limiting features, be serving as a gateway to not only a physical place, but also one of spirituality? Maybe its narrowness served to cleanse someone's energy before they entered a sacred area. I know mine felt lighter after walking through it.

As we exited the tunnel and entered the main chamber, I became aware of a change in the energy of the cave. There was a deep quiet, but also a deeper vibrancy in the air that I hadn't experienced in any of the other caves I'd explored while spelunking. I couldn't pinpoint what I was feeling, but with patience and time the secrets of Gost Cave might be revealed to me. My guides told me to settle in, relax, and go with the energetic flow of the cave. In other words, I was to allow my energy to vibrate and merge with the energy around me.

Calming my energy down, I followed David and Beth over to the wall where the carvings were. There, in high relief, was the face of a man sculpted out of the calcite wall. Next to the human face was the carved head of a jaguar with eyes staring out at us. Was the positioning of the two faces side by side meant to show two beings existing in one guise? The human priest or shaman shapeshifting into his more powerful form, the great cat? Maybe the jaguar here represented the jaguar deity worshipped throughout the Americas by ancient priests and shamans and disciples. After all, ancient (as well as present-day) worshippers believed the jaguar was able to move back and forth between the shadows of the Underworld and the world of the living. For those who were worthy, the jaguar was a powerful ally and protector of the priests and shamans as they worked with otherworldly powers and the Underworld. Through this alliance, they were able to walk safely and fearlessly in the realms of the supernatural while gathering great knowledge. It wasn't by accident that the jaguar had been elevated by ancient priests and shamans to the high honor of being the primary animal form the god Tezcatlipoca manifested himself as.

All of this was going through my mind as we studied the two enigmatic faces. They stared back at us in mute refusal to yield their secrets. Leaving the carvings behind, we set off to explore other areas of the cave.

Some of the cave walls had beautiful, glistening, multi-colored calcite deposits that sparkled from the moisture seeping down through the earth above us. Beth, the ever-ready photographer, got the great cave photos she had hoped to get.

As we continued walking through the rooms, I became aware of a beauty in the cave's quietude and simplicity that reminded me of the holy energy I always felt at one of my favorite locations in New Orleans, the Archbishop's Chapel at the old Ursuline Convent. And like that chapel, despite its simplicity and quietude, or rather because of it, there was a great and powerful energy throbbing all around us.

We were not alone.

The presence of the facilitators of this energy were beginning to manifest all around us. In actuality, what was going on was that, by relaxing and allowing my energy to flow, I was getting on the same energetic frequency as the cave and its supernatural beings. I could feel my energy being drawn into, merging with, this mass of otherworldly energy. I could hear the cave whispering over and over, "Welcome, welcome!"

Putting out my hand, I touched its wall. A throbbing energy passed into my hand and through my body. I could now hear these ancient ones chanting over and over, protecting this sacred place with the energy of their voices.

The throbbing I heard and felt throughout the cave was emanating from the low hum created by their continual chanting.

Then I saw them! My energetic frequency had risen to match the level of their frequency. The holy men—priests—were sitting cross legged throughout the rooms of the cave. They were sitting bare legged and bare chested on the damp earth. Their dedication to their mission, to the exclusion of all else, reminded me of the individuals who belong to some of the world's religions who dedicate themselves to a life of celibacy, meditation, and prayer. By doing so, they believe they're serving as power sources for their organizations. The priests/shamans here in Gost Cave appeared to be doing much the same thing. There was one big difference between the former and the latter, though. Unlike the former, the priests/shamans here in Gost Cave were dead, at least in the physical sense.

They were the ghosts of the ancient ones who had inhabited this sacred cave eons ago. They were still doing in death what they had done in life: serving as conduits for the energy of their Earth Mother as she nourished her children.

The ghost priests all around us were so focused on their mission, in fact, they appeared oblivious to our presence. I wasn't going to get any help from these otherworldly priests.

Just then, I sensed a presence behind me. Turning around, I saw the ghost of a short, powerfully built young man standing near the carvings. Unlike the ghost priests, he was definitely aware of our presence, for he was avidly watching our every move.

Could this be the presence that David had felt watching him on his earlier visits to the cave, and who had later followed him home? Why were he and these other ghosts from a much more ancient time still here? What had happened to these ancient people? Once again, as is usually the case when I'm on an otherworldly adventure, my curiosity came to the fore. Determined to satisfy it, if the ghost priest would cooperate, I slowly approached him and sat on a large rock. I waited as he studied me, more from interest than alarm.

Finally, the ghost broke the silence between us, asking me with keen interest, "You're not like the others who have come to the sacred cave. You can see us. How is this?"

He stood there, arms crossed across his bare chest, expectantly waiting for my answer. I could tell that he was going to want his questions answered if he was going to answer mine. How to explain my abilities to this ancient being, though? Then my wise main spirit guide, Black Hawk, said, "Keep it simple, Boo. It's not complicated how your abilities work."

Taking a deep, calming breath, I told him, "Because I can work with my energy I, like you, am able to travel between the different realms of existence. This enables me to make connections with other beings."

"How are you able to communicate with me?" he asked.

Black Hawk then told me to ask him if he could talk to the birds.

"Yes, of course!" he answered. "We talk to all our brothers and sisters, all the children of Mother Earth."

"How do you do this?" I asked.

"We're all One Spirit in different forms," he stated. "Because we're all from the same energy Source, our different physical forms don't block us from merging, blending our energies with different beings if we want to."

Hmm, I thought. *Said much better than I ever put it.*

Once again he quietly studied me, still waiting for my response. I was ready this time, though. "You have answered your own question as to how I'm able to see and communicate with you. I can do it because we're all One in Spirit. I can match my energy with yours, but only for a brief time. Otherwise my physical body becomes tired from the energy drain. Right now my energy is blending with yours."

At getting his question answered, a small smile of satisfaction crossed his face, giving me tacit permission to now ask my questions.

Eagerly, I asked, "Who are you? Why are you and the other ghosts here in this cave? Do you know you're dead?" (Okay, so I'm not the most patient type after all!)

With a tolerant smile, the young ghost priest explained, "I'm an acolyte in training to the priests here in this sacred cave. We serve Mother Earth. Yes, we know we have passed from the physical realm into the realm of spirits. This change of form doesn't change our agreement with Mother Earth to serve and protect her, though. We must fulfill this agreement at all costs!"

"Who are your people? What happened to them?"

"The people of my village and our other villages are long gone. Many, many lifetimes ago my people lived throughout the grasslands and the mountains of this land. Others of our people lived by the big water. Our ancestors came from a rich and powerful land far to the west and south. It was a land of violence and conquests.

"No one was safe. Our religion allowed for no other way to live. My ancestors broke away from the violent practices of their old religion, leaving their homeland behind. They left to find a better way to live. They had realized that the harsh, violent nature of their former religion sowed only disharmony and imbalance. Because of this, there was always chaos throughout the land. With their move, their vision of harmony came to pass. They, and their new way of life, spread from west to east.

"Now you call us the ancient ones. When we were alive, we were called the People of Peace. We were powerful healers. Our priests possessed great knowledge about things that are no longer known to your world." (At his words concerning our lack of knowledge of these powerful, magical forces, I couldn't help but think that maybe our ignorance concerning these forces was a blessing in disguise. There's an old saying: "Ignorance is bliss." Well, in this case, ignorance might be protection. Who knows what uncontrollable forces might be unleashed if this ancient knowledge fell into the wrong hands, given the age we now live in.)

Aware of but untouched by my cynical thoughts concerning my own time, the acolyte kept going with his narrative. "The priests lived in sacred caves so they could be surrounded by powerful earth energies as they practiced their magic. The mountain around this cave made earth energy even more powerful. Also, by being inside the earth, the priests could be closer to the Underworld.

"The sacred cave was kept safe from impure energy. The only ones ever allowed near the cave, and to come in, were us young acolytes. Each priest had an acolyte that waited on him and was being trained by him. This training ensured that there was always somebody to replace a priest when he died.

"The village below our mountain kept the priests and acolytes fed. There was only one path up the mountain to the cave. This the villagers used to bring the food to the acolytes. The acolytes would then carry it in to the priests. While they ate, we acolytes would take over the chanting. We also guarded the sacred cave and the priests.

"In return for the peoples' care, the priests used their ancient knowledge to bring Mother Earth's blessings to them. They acted as conduits for Her energy. Through the priests' partnership with Mother Earth, they could work with powerful, magical forces that enabled them to control the weather, work with unpredictable forces from other realms to gain knowledge, and to affect the life force—energy—of the organic matter around them, such as animals, plants, and people. By manipulating this energy, they could cause them to flourish or to decay.

"All organic matter flourished and prospered under the benign magic of our priests. The crops were good and game was plentiful. No one went hungry. We stayed in harmony with Mother Earth. All was in balance and good. It was a time of peace among the people of the east and west. The energy of Mother Earth ensured this. Other priests and shamans worked with her energy as we did. We shared our great knowledge with all who wanted to learn. Mother Earth's energy brought goodness to the people far and wide."

I sat spellbound as I listened to the ghost acolyte describe the magical, utopian world he had lived in. His face shone with joy as he relived his story. Suddenly, he paused. A shadow chased the joy from his countenance. Was that a tear slowly rolling down his cheek? I could not be sure, as the shadows and gloom seemed to have deepened around him. Obviously the next part of his story was painful for him to relive.

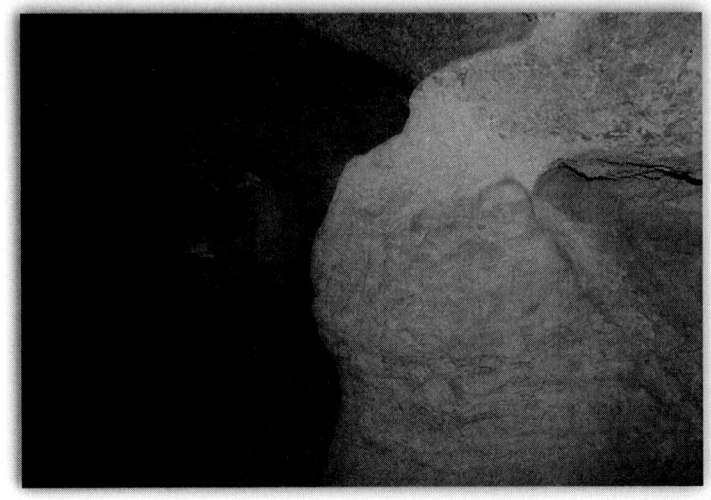

*Boo channeling the acolyte ghost
beside the stone carvings in Gost Cave*

He continued to sit in silence, wrapped in the cloak of his pain. Would he finish his story? I looked to Black Hawk for answers about the situation. Knowing my restive nature, he silently held a finger up to his lips and telepathically told me to be patient. I waited, now knowing that the ghost needed time to gather himself. In all the eons he'd existed as a ghost in the cave, he'd never had the opportunity to tell anyone his story before. He'd never had to relive it as he was now doing by telling it. Finally, he appeared composed enough to continue his narrative.

I prodded him further by gently asking him, "What happened to your people, your way of life?"

"The sickness came," he stated with a deep sigh of resignation. "It was brought from the north. The peoples to the north always came in peace to our villages to gain wisdom and to trade, but they were always fighting among themselves. There was chaos and imbalance around them from the imbalanced energy of their violent lives. They, and we, didn't realize it, but they brought the sickness with them to our people. The people in the villages got sick and began dying. They brought the sickness to the acolytes when they brought the priests' food. The acolytes, not realizing what they were doing, carried not only the food of life to the priests, but also death. The sickness happened quickly. The priests began to die in the sacred cave."

The ghost acolyte's words spilled out faster and faster, as if he couldn't bring his story to its tragic end soon enough.

"The acolytes were dying also, and so there was no one to replace the priests as they died. The energy of their chants became weaker and weaker, making it harder to harness Mother Earth's energy. The sickness killed off villages far and wide. When our village died, there was no one left to bring us food. We chose to stay anyway because the chanting must not be allowed to fall silent. Eventually we starved to death. But even in death, we will not leave. We will chant for eternity if we must to protect all of the children of Mother Earth."

Remembering what David had told me, that there had been no record of human remains found in Gost Cave, I now asked the ghost, "If you died here in the cave, and all died around you, where are the bodies?"

"Others of our kind journeyed from far away to gather our bodies and carry them away to give them proper burial, to return them to Mother Earth. By burying our bodies, they gave back to Mother Earth what was hers, our physical forms. Even in life, we didn't take from her. We took only what she was willing to give. She is wise and knows how to keep her children and herself in balance and harmony. To take from Mother Earth with disrespect throws everything out of balance. Then the world and its inhabitants are thrown into chaos and disharmony.

"There are magical forces for great good that your people have become unaware of. In the ignorance of your age, your people don't even believe in these forces. How is this so? Are not these forces all around you? The people of your time are blind and Mother Earth suffers because of this blindness. This is why we can't move on, because Mother Earth still needs us. We're keepers of Mother Earth. We serve the Mother—Mother Earth. Only in this way will we be able to help bring the Great Peace back to our brothers and sisters far and wide."

The acolyte paused once again, waiting for my response. Instead, I turned to Black Hawk for affirmation of what I had picked up a bit earlier. "They're not ready to move on, cross over, are they?"

"No."

I felt a sadness at the thought of the ghost priests staying trapped. Because of the spirit bond between us, Black Hawk felt my sadness. "Black Panther," he said, calling me by my spirit name instead of my Earth Realm name, Boo. It's the name he knew me by when we were together in past lives. "Don't feel sad for them. They'll be fine. They don't see themselves as trapped, but fulfilling a mission for your planet, Mother Earth. Until the inhabitants of your planet change and shift to a higher level of consciousness, these ancient ones will keep their vigil for Her."

Accepting the wisdom of Black Hawk's words, and comforted by them, I turned back one last time to the young ghost acolyte. Quietly, he told me, "Remember, Black Panther, you too have your own way of working with Mother Earth, as do others of your time. Tell the man called David in this life that he was chosen to live many lives in the Earth Realm to help spread the message of peace and love and goodness for all beings. Even though he no longer chants with his brothers, he will always be one of us, and is always welcome. Now go in peace, for we are tired."

Before I had a chance to thank the ghost acolyte for sharing his wisdom, he gave me a gentle smile, turned, and walked away. I watched him as he once again moved among the seated, chanting priests, taking care of their needs. Mother Earth was in good hands.

I walked over to join David and Beth where they had been patiently waiting by the tunnel entrance. It was time to leave the cave and its ghosts to their vigil. Up the rope we went, out of Gost Cave, and into the brightness of a beautiful afternoon.

As we made our way back down the mountain, I turned to take one last look at the sacred cave—not to tell it goodbye, but that I would be back for another visit at another time. A visit that would allow me to once again bask in the beautiful, benevolent energy of the Guardians of Gost Cave.

THE LIGHTHOUSE KEEPER WHO NEVER LEFT

Cape San Blas, located on the St. Joseph peninsula, is a little piece of paradise found in the Florida panhandle. Its beach has been consistently ranked in the top ten in the nation. Its sands are snow white and the Gulf is rather calm in this area of the coastline. Until recently, this stretch of Florida coastline remained undiscovered by developers and tourists. This suited the local populace, as they were satisfied with their easygoing way of life. A lot of them are descended from the original settlers who came into this area in 1835. These settlers called their town St. Joseph. It was a remote settlement on Florida's frontier. It was later renamed Port St. Joe after a yellow-fever epidemic decimated a large portion of the original population in the 1840s.

The people today, like their ancestors years ago, still enjoy living off the rich bounties of the land and water by using their fishing and hunting skills. Until recently, there was also steady employment with the biggest employer in the area, the St. Joe Company. The St. Joe Company was a paper mill that churned out paper products by the ton. Needing trees for its paper production, it owned most of the large tracts of land in the area. This ensured an endless supply of pulpwood.

However, the paper mill caused a lot of environmental pollution and damage to the land and water in the Port St. Joe–Cape San Blas area. But as is so true in life, there's always a flip side to the coin. The positive consequence of the mill's presence was that developers hungry for coastal land to exploit were kept out of the area. There simply was no land available to develop. The paper company owned everything.

Everything changed when, in 1998, the St. Joe paper mill shut down. As a result, many people lost their jobs and the area's economy suffered. But because of its beautiful beaches and native charm, the area was able to turn to tourism to help soften the economic blow dealt it when the mill closed.

The beautiful beaches are not the only attractions drawing people to the area. The fishing is superb on this section of the coastline. There's also the beautiful St. Joseph Peninsula State Park. It's one of the most popular state parks in Florida. Its beaches and big dunes have been zealously maintained in their original, pristine condition. Here visitors can see how the original Florida coastline looked before the big, protective dunes in other areas were knocked down and flattened to make way for rampant development. The park is also home to a vast array of indigenous wildlife that visitors can observe and study.

Another main attraction not to be missed is the famous Cape San Blas Lighthouse with its two keepers' cottages. The lighthouse was born out of necessity in the 1800s. The Cape San Blas coastal area, despite its welcoming beauty, has always been an extremely dangerous place for ships. The danger comes from a huge shoal offshore that has been the destruction and death of many ships and their crews and passengers. This was especially true in the 1800s and early 1900s. A lighthouse was needed to warn ships away when they were sailing or steaming too close to this fatal underwater hazard.

Cape San Blas Lighthouse with its two keeper's cottages and the oil house

The first Cape San Blas lighthouse was erected in 1849. It stood until 1851, when it was destroyed by a gale. It was replaced in 1856 by a similar brick tower, but this second lighthouse was destroyed by a hurricane a few months later. The third Cape San Blas lighthouse was built in 1857, but was damaged by Confederate troops during the Civil War. It survived the damage only to be toppled by beach erosion in 1882. It seems that the San Blas coastline has not only been a hazardous place for ships, but also its lighthouses.

Yet the United States government persevered, and so the fourth one, the present lighthouse, was built in 1883. It's a ninety-eight-foot-tall, skeletal-type lighthouse composed of eight cast-iron legs that support the watch room and lantern at the top of the tower. The current keepers' cottages were completed in 1905. The lighthouse and its keepers' cottages have seen many tenders and visitors come and go over the years. There was one lighthouse keeper, though, who came but never left, at least in spirit.

I encountered this ghost of the Cape San Blas Lighthouse while on a trip to the cape with my good friend Beth. She's a lighthouse aficionado. Wherever she travels, she seeks out the local lighthouse. The Cape San Blas Lighthouse was no exception.

It was a beautiful spring day when we took a break from the beach to visit it. Photography is another passion of Beth's, and according to professional, expert sources, she's quite talented at it. She was excited because she said the lighting at this time of day was perfect to capture a stunning photo of the lighthouse. Now Beth, when photographing, bears a resemblance to me when I'm working with ghosts; she's totally immersed in it. So we separated, Beth to take photos and me to see what adventures I could get myself into. Adventures of the more ghostly kind, I might add, for earlier, while gathering information about the area from some of the local residents, they had mentioned the magic word: haunted!

"Oh, you must check out the old Cape San Blas Lighthouse. It's haunted!" was the unanimous refrain.

They had then proceeded to tell me about different incidences witnessed and experienced at the old lighthouse over the years that left no doubt it was occupied by an otherworldly type. One such incident witnessed many times involves the lighthouse's lantern. The Cape San Blas Lighthouse was deactivated and its lantern extinguished in 1996. With the lighthouse keeper no longer there to look after it, the lighthouse had fallen into an advanced state of disrepair, making it impossible for its lantern to operate.

Despite this apparent impossibility, many people throughout the years tell of seeing the lantern still shining brightly on dark, cloudy nights. When they drive out to check on the old, locked-up lighthouse, the lantern is dark and there's no one there—at least no one they can see.

Another odd incident that has been experienced many times by visitors who come to the lighthouse involves the mysterious footsteps they hear ringing on the metal stairwell as they climb the lighthouse. The visitors don't think much about the footsteps until they reach the top or descend to the bottom, where they suddenly realize that they were the only ones in the old lighthouse at the time.

Sailors out at sea have reported seeing the lighthouse functioning as it had in its working past, bright light shining. They've even watched as the figure of a man ascends and descends the lighthouse's metal stairway, the glow from the swinging lantern he carries bathing him in its yellow light. After descending the lighthouse, the mysterious figure is then seen walking up and down the beach, still swinging the bright lantern in warning. Then he just disappears.

Who's this apparition? My loquacious local informants told me that it's believed to be the restless spirit of Ernest W. Marler, an assistant lighthouse keeper who was murdered in 1938 by an unknown assailant. His murder has never been solved despite the fact that it was a violent, gruesome one.

According to all individuals at the time, Marler by repute had been a decent man with a bright future in front of him. He had been a likable young man in his thirties. No one could think of any known enemies he might have had. That is why, because of its senseless nature, his murder had been such a shock at the time.

Marler's murder occurred sometime on the morning of March 16, 1938. On this day, as on all other days while employed as assistant keeper, he had gone to tend the lighthouse in the early morning. Then it was his habit to be in his workshop located behind his cottage by 10:00 a.m. Here, he would work on finishing up projects until the early afternoon, when he would return home for lunch. This day was to play out differently, though—horribly different!

When Marler didn't return home for lunch as he always did, his wife, Susie, sent one of their young daughters to tell her father lunch was ready. The little girl ran right into the gruesome scene of her slaughtered father. Frightened and not understanding what she had seen, she ran home crying, telling her mother, "Daddy is hurt! Go and help him!"

Mrs. Marler rushed to the workshop, unprepared for the grisly scene that awaited her. She found her husband at the end of his workbench, his body lying in a large pool of blood. He had fourteen stab wounds around the heart and a fifteenth slashing his neck. His left wrist had been cut so deeply that the nearly severed hand dangled at his side.

Hearing her cries for help, Culligan Reynolds, the head lighthouse keeper, was one of the first to arrive on the scene. He quickly told the other witnesses that Marler had committed suicide. But when the sheriff arrived, he changed Reynolds's ruling to murder. He stated that it would be impossible to self-inflict such wounds as Marler's body had sustained. In fact, the wounds were so deep, the mortician later stated he had had trouble embalming the body. The murder weapons, a bloody knife and hatchet, were found two feet from the body. Despite being sent away to check for fingerprints, they led to no suspects.

It's been seventy-six years since the murder, and yet the cold case continues to fascinate the area. I myself was fascinated with it and the possibility that the ghost of the murder victim might still be roaming the site of his horrible, gruesome demise. As anyone who knows me will tell you, Boo's curiosity is ever smoldering. So it doesn't take much to ignite it! Such was the case now as I hurried to see the person who might be able to help me satisfy it, Beverly Douds.

Beverly is the curator and caretaker of the Cape San Blas Lighthouse. I found her in the gift shop helping customers. I waited for her to finish and then introduced myself. "Hi, my name is Boo."

"I'm Beverly," she responded. "Is Boo your real name? That's an odd name, don't you think?"

Ah, I thought, *a person who gets right to the point and is not afraid to speak her mind.* Forthrightness is a trait I've always admired in people because you always know where they stand.

"Yes, that's my name," I replied in amusement. "I was given the name Boo when I was a three-day-old baby. And as you can see by looking at me, I've had it a long time!" I said with a laugh.

Now, with the ice broken between us and the name thing out of the way, I could get right to my purpose for being here: ghosts! Cautiously, for one never knows whose skeptical or religious toes one might trod upon by bringing up this potentially touchy subject, I led off with, "Beverly, some of the people around have been telling me about unusual goings-on here at your lighthouse. They believe there's a ghost hanging around it. Do you know anything about it?"

In her usual forthright manner, she informed me, "Well, strange things do happen at this lighthouse all the time, such as footsteps and other noises that can't be explained. And there have been several odd deaths that have occurred here over the years. But I don't think one way or the other about there being any ghosts hereabouts. Even if there were, they wouldn't concern me!"

I could believe this. It would have to be one serious, bad-butt ghost if it were going to get Beverly's attention. No ordinary variety of ghost could manage it! She would walk right over it, or rather through it, and keep going. I guess if you had grown up like Beverly had, with alligators and rattlesnakes using your front yard as a highway, it would tend to put most ghostly issues in perspective.

During our exchange, Beverly came across as a no-nonsense individual encased in a tough exterior. To the eyes of the astute and perceptive, though, the shining gleam from a heart of gold could be glimpsed. Not only does Beverly have a generous heart, but she also possesses a great love of learning that has driven her to become an accomplished amateur historian and genealogist. Little escapes her notice, and she's used these skills to help her write and publish several historical books about the area.

It was this love of history that drove her, along with several others, to spearhead the effort to save the old Cape San Blas Lighthouse. Without their dedicated and determined efforts to save and restore the lighthouse, it would have been allowed to fall into the surf to its destruction a long time ago. Instead, because of Beverly and her group's unremitting belief in the historical importance of the lighthouse to their area, they raised the funds to restore it. Their efforts were so determined, in fact, they also managed to raise the funds needed to restore the lighthouse's two keepers' cottages as well. One of the cottages served as living quarters for the head keeper and his family. The second cottage was used to house the assistant keeper and his family. Nowadays the head keeper's cottage is a gift shop for the lighthouse. The assistant keeper's cottage was still going through renovations to make it ready to house the lighthouse museum.

This second cottage was the one I was interested in. I'd caught a glimpse of a shadowy something, or someone, moving around the cottage when Beth and I had driven up. I told Beverly about the movement and asked her permission to check out the cottage to see what, or rather who, I might run into. Now I knew already from the way Beverly talked that she was skeptical about ghosts but also inquisitive by nature, making her my favorite kind of skeptic: open minded! And so, with an amused smile, she granted my request, telling me, "Sure Boo, knock yourself out! Let me know if you find anything or anyone." She chuckled. "I'll radio my son Frank so he can unlock the cottage." With that, she turned back to help a customer who had walked in the door.

I met Frank at the assistant keeper's cottage as Beth arrived from the lighthouse.

"What's up?" she asked.

"I'm going into the cottage to see if I can locate the lighthouse ghost. I believe he's the one I saw hanging around here earlier."

"Oh wow, can I go in too?" Beth asked Frank.

I couldn't help but laugh at her excitement about going into the old cottage. "You mean to help find the ghost, or to see the cottage with its artifacts?" I asked. To be honest, ghosts don't get Beth excited in the least. History does.

Now with Beth in tow, Frank and I proceeded up the steps to the porch. As we stepped upon it, there he was! From the intense way he stared at me, I could tell that he was aware I could see him. I whispered to Beth, "The ghost is here. I want to wait for him in the parlor." Frank unlocked the door and we walked inside. I knew that the entity would follow. Sure enough, we had barely sat on the antique sofa when there he was, materializing in the doorway of the kitchen.

There was blood all over the front of his neck and striped white shirt. His right hand grasped his bloody left wrist and hand in desperation, holding them as if in an attempt to keep them from falling apart. (I have seen quite a few bloody ghosts over the years, but he had to be one of the more gruesome.)

"Ah, the lighthouse ghost is Marler," I exclaimed to Beth. Just to be sure, I asked the ghost his name and why he was still here.

"I'm Ernest Marler. I was the assistant lighthouse keeper here until I was murdered in 1938."

"So, you're aware you're dead?" I asked.

"Yes," he stated with a total lack of emotion.

A most unusual reaction, I thought. Many times when someone is killed by violence, their spirit will harbor a strong desire for revenge upon the perpetrator. The only feelings I detected around Marler were sadness, guilt, and a resignation over his self-inflicted entrapment in the Ghost Realm. I say self-inflicted because no one else can cause a spirit to be trapped in the Ghost Realm. It's the deceased's decision, even if they don't realize this at the time they're making it. This self-entrapment is something a spirit does to itself when it holds on too stubbornly to earthly issues such as revenge, lost or unrequited love, guilt, regret, fear of judgment, and so on.

Because of the unresolved issue being obsessed over, the restless deceased dies with the strong yearning for more time in the human life. This yearning comes from the mistaken belief that if they had this extra time they could change the outcome to their satisfaction. They want more time in the physical to make different choices to create a different ending to the issue. And yet, it just doesn't work like that. What you don't change or resolve in the earthly realm, you rarely can change in death. As a consequence of not realizing this, they trap themselves in an existence of illusion while trying to resolve the issue from the wrong realm.

Marler was trapped in the Ghost Realm and knew it, so what was holding him there? As if reading my thoughts (which he was probably doing already), his next words drew me out of my musings.

"I blame myself, you know," he stated.

"What do you blame yourself for?" I asked, startled by this declaration from a victim of a violent crime. One would expect the perpetrator to be blamed, to bear the burden of guilt, not the victim!

"For being killed!" he answered. "It was my fault! I was a decent young man with a wife and family. I liked my job and was giving my family a decent living. I threw it all away in a moment's weakness. I should have known better than to do what I did. I threw it all away, all away!" he exclaimed in despair, emotion showing for the first time. He paused for a moment as tears of sorrow streamed down his face. Overwhelmed and embarrassed by his emotion, he quickly turned away.

Fearing he was about to leave, I regained his attention with, "Mr. Marler, your death has remained a mystery for many years. Would you please tell me what happened? Why you blame yourself for your violent demise?"

The ghost turned back to me with an air of resignation. "Okay, what difference does it make now? I was Mr. Reynolds's assistant. He was the head keeper of the lighthouse. He was all right to work for when he wasn't drinking, which was most of the time. I suspect he had dealings with the illegal bootleggers in the area. We were always told to look out for these smugglers, but we never seemed to be able to catch any of them at their illegal activities.

"He could also have a quick temper on occasion. Because of his drinking, I usually ended up with more than my fair share of the work of running the lighthouse. Our job was to make sure the light was always burning. I took this responsibility seriously, even if he didn't. Men's lives were depending on the lighthouse operating.

"Mr. Reynolds could be something of a bully too, especially after he'd given in to his weakness for the bottle. Despite this, he usually treated me decently. This decency didn't extend to his wife, Miss Velma, though. Because of his jealousy, many's the time the peace of the morning or evening would be disturbed by their loud arguing. He would be yelling at her and she would be screaming back. Then would come the sound of blows landing. Afterward he would come storming out of the house, driving away angrily.

"My wife, Susie, would then go over to make sure Miss Velma was all right. One afternoon, though, after one really bad argument, Susie was unable to go because of looking after our youngest, who was sick in bed. So she sent me instead.

"I found Miss Velma sitting on the bed upstairs, holding her bruised face in her hands. Startled by my sudden appearance, she turned away in an attempt to hide the bruises. Uncomfortable with the situation, I asked her if she was all right. She didn't seem to hear me, so I stepped to her side to ask again. Before I was aware of her intent, she got up and flung her arms around my neck! I stood there in shock, not knowing what to do.

"As she cried on my shoulder, she exclaimed in anguish how she hated her husband and that she wished something bad would happen to him. She also said that he was jealous of me for being a vigorous, young man. 'Many's the time he's accused me of looking at you—that there's something going on between us. And maybe there is!' she said.

"I should have paid more attention to what she was saying. Instead, I looked down at her in shocked disbelief as she looked up. I noticed the tears were gone just before she gave me a hard, hungry kiss. Taken by surprise, I responded to her desperate passion, but then I tried to pull away. She was relentless, though, holding me tightly to her. Before I knew it, we were on the bed and I had almost broken my marriage vows!

"Just in time, I pulled away from Miss Velma in self-disgust, but the damage was done. I was so filled with shame and guilt, I couldn't even look at her. As I hurried for the door, she exclaimed, 'You'll be back!' Was that a note of triumph in her voice? I couldn't say for sure, I was so young and naive.

"When I got back to my cottage, Susie asked how Miss Velma was and what had taken so long. I tried to hide the shameful incident so as to spare Susie, but I have always been an honest man. Seeing the guilt and shame on my face and my disheveled appearance, she asked me, 'What have you done, Ernest? What have you done?'

"My silence and guilty face proclaimed all. Susie broke down crying. I tried to hold her to comfort her, telling her over and over how sorry I was and that it didn't mean a thing to me. She rejected me in deep hurt, pushing me away. Running into the bedroom, she slammed the door and locked it.

"As I sat in the kitchen waiting for her to come out, I could hear her crying. I felt such deep shame and guilt and anger toward myself for my momentary weakness. I did love her, and she me." As the ghost said this, tears of remorse streamed down his pale face once again. Trying to wipe the tears away with a shrug of his injured right shoulder, he continued his tragic story. "Finally, the bedroom door opened and she stepped out, dry eyed. 'For the sake of the children, we will never speak of this again!' she said. 'We will try to put it behind us and move on.'

"With that she coldly turned away, ignoring me as she started supper. The next few days were rough between us. Despite the coldness from Susie, I had hope that things would work out.

"And so they would have if Miss Velma hadn't come to my workshop a week later. Entering, she shut the door behind her. Upon seeing who my visitor was, I stood and stepped a respectable distance away from her. Frowning at my reaction, she crossed her arms and got right to the point. 'What are we going to do about the situation between us?' she asked.

" 'There's no situation between us. It'll never happen again!' I stated firmly.

" 'Oh, yes there is!' she shot back. 'I know you're attracted to me and so does my husband!'

" 'Why would he think this?' I wondered. But in my confusion and discomfort with Miss Velma's presence, I didn't ask her this as I should have. I just wanted her gone before Susie saw her. So, in my haste to have her gone, I stepped around her and opened the door, asking her to leave.

"Anger at my rejection crossed her face. 'You'll be sorry!' she spat at me as she turned and stalked out. I turned back into my workshop thinking that everything would be okay with time. Little did I know that there would soon be no more time for me. As I have said before, I was a naive, young man.

"One morning soon after, I heard the Reynolds arguing as I walked by on my way to my workshop. I paid them no mind, as I wanted no trouble. I was also hurrying to finish up a project before lunch because I had promised Susie, in an attempt to make up for my hurtful action, that I would help her with some chores that afternoon. This was why I was hurrying to finish by lunchtime. I didn't want to cause her any more upset by being late.

"With this thought in mind, and concentrating on the repair job at hand, I didn't hear the heavy footsteps outside the shed. I was bent over my work when, the next thing I knew, the door was flung open with a bang and Mr. Reynolds rushed in! I straightened up, thinking he needed my help with an emergency of some kind. He came at me so quickly that it wasn't until he was almost on top of me that I saw the knife in his hand.

"Grabbing the hatchet off the table, he screamed at me, 'What is this about you and my wife?' In the heat and anger of the argument, she had thrown in his face what had happened between us! At his words, the look of guilt that crossed my face sealed my fate. Enraged, he rushed at me with the knife, striking viciously! I threw up my left arm to defend myself. The knife slashed deeply into my wrist and hand. The pain was excruciating. I grabbed them with my right hand and tried to get away.

"He rushed after me! Catching me at the workbench, he swung the hatchet at my head. I dodged but it caught me in the throat, cutting it. I fell to the floor in a great agony of pain and terror over my wounds. The fact that I was now totally helpless to defend myself against his insane attack terrified me and sent me into a state of panic! My will to live was so strong, I grabbed the bench leg with my right hand and dragged my body over to it. My one thought was to get to the door to somehow escape.

"With this in mind, I kept trying to pull my body up by using the bench leg. In panicked desperation, I tried over and over to pull myself up. But my bloody right hand kept slipping down the wooden leg. The last thing I remember before I blacked out from the terrible pain was Mr. Reynolds bending over me, face contorted by his insane rage as he stabbed me with the knife, driving it over and over into my chest.

"The next thing I felt was a sense of lightness. I was now looking down at my body being stabbed, but I felt no pain. Mr. Reynolds was gasping and there was blood all over his shirt and pants. My blood! What had happened to me? What had he done to me? The bloody, mutilated object that had once been my body told the story.

"All of a sudden, Mr. Reynolds came to his senses, looking around in panic. 'What have I done?' he exclaimed as he backed away from my lifeless body. Then, answering his own question, he spat out, 'Well, the bastard deserved it, he did!'

"Throwing down the bloody murder weapons, he started to turn away. But then a change came over him. He had impulsively attacked me in the heat of his rage. Now that this rage had been spent, his rational mind reasserted itself. He realized the murder weapons could be traced back to him. I watched as he picked them up and wiped away his bloody fingerprints with a rag from my workbench.

"Then, going to the door, he furtively looked around and strode out. As I now had nothing to fear, I followed him. He grabbed a shovel that was leaning against the shed wall. Walking deep into the woods, he dug a hole and buried his bloody shirt. Then he calmly walked back to his house as if nothing had happened. As he walked through the door, his wife looked up in fear and alarm. As she saw the flecks of blood on his pants, I heard her think to herself in shock, 'It was supposed to be you!' When I heard her, I realized that ghosts can hear the thoughts of the living if they care to.

"Mr. Reynolds glared at her for a long moment. Not a word was exchanged between them, but I knew she had an idea as to what had happened. I could feel her fear of him as she looked at him in dread. He wasn't supposed to be the one to return. She had hoped I would take care of her husband for her when he confronted me about our 'involvement.' She had set me up!

"How naive and trusting I had been! But she was not to go unpunished for her scheming. Her plan had backfired. She now had to live with a much worse version of her abusive husband than the original. He had proven himself a killer, and now she was bound to him even more firmly because she had been part of it, if only indirectly.

"I felt no satisfaction, though, from the thought of her having to pay for her part in bringing about my death. In fact, I felt nothing as I watched him, after giving her one last glare of warning to keep her mouth shut, stomp up the stairs to wash my blood off of himself. I then returned to the shed where my body lay. I was there when my little girl came skipping in to call me to lunch. She gave a frightened cry when she saw my body and then ran out screaming for her mama. The guilt from not being able to take her in my arms and comfort her, to make her feel safe, was almost overwhelming!

"Instead, I continued to stand next to my body. I didn't know where else to go. I couldn't go to my wife and daughters—they were too grief stricken. Their sadness made me feel so guilty for no longer being there to support them and look after them.

"Then, after a while, I didn't even have my body. Some men came and took it away for burial. Feeling lost, I went to the inquest into my murder. Nothing came of it, though. Susie had been too scared and ashamed to speak up about what had happened between Miss Velma and me. Besides, not suspecting Mr. Reynolds, she saw no reason to. This would have provided a motive, bringing attention to him.

"As it was, after his quick attempt to have my death ruled a suicide failed, he then blamed it on unknown criminals. I yelled, 'Liar!' but of course no one heard me. No one listens to a ghost! After the failed inquest, all I had left was the lighthouse. That is where I stayed from then on.

"Mr. Reynolds, after his unsuccessful attempt to have the case closed by having my death ruled a suicide, left the San Blas Lighthouse a few months later. The reason he gave for his abrupt departure was that he was afraid for his life. He claimed the murderer might come back. The only real fear he had was that his terrible deed would come to light with time.

"Well, there was also the matter of me haunting him! Having no place else to go, and being duty bound to protect the lives of the men at sea, I stayed close to the lighthouse. This meant I stayed close to Mr. Reynolds also. He was drinking more now and not fulfilling his duties as he should.

"That's why I stayed instead of following him when he left. I intended to still do my job even if he wasn't going to do his. Why should the seamen pay with their lives just because he had destroyed mine? No, I would never let them down like I had my family! I must stay here to make sure the lighthouse is always lit and operating properly."

I asked him if he was aware the Cape San Blas Lighthouse was now automated and serving as a tourist attraction.

"Yes, I know this," he stated. "This doesn't free me from my duties, though. I never got to fulfill them because my murder cut my time here short. I must still carry out my duties until they're completed."

"How will you know when they're completed so you will be free to leave the Ghost Realm?" I asked in an attempt to help him straighten out his twisted logic.

"I don't know. I just know I have to do my job. I can't let anyone down now like I did in life!"

Ah, the typical ghostly confusion, I thought, *creating an issue from the twisted logic of an obsession that results in trapping the spirit.* In Marler's case, the obsession, or issue, was extreme guilt.

I could see the conundrum he had created for himself by his obsessive need to right the "wrong" (as he saw it) he had done to his loved ones while alive. But, as is usually the case when one is a ghost, he was in the wrong realm to do this. Marler's obsessive guilt was making it hard for him to see this, though. In his confusion he saw the lighthouse, not the Other Side, as the place that would enable him to make up for his mistakes while alive.

Keeping this confusion of his in mind, I started to ask the ghost more questions in an attempt to help him find clarity with his situation. This clarity and understanding would hopefully help him decide to cross over to the Other Side, where peace awaited. But before I could question him further, he turned to leave. I tried to forestall him. "Mr. Marler, where are you going?"

"I must go finish some repairs. I've wasted enough time!" he answered, once again focusing on his illusional "duty," keeping the Cape San Blas Lighthouse working. Then, without so much as a goodbye, he vanished into thin air.

Caught by surprise by the ghost's unexpected exit, I could only stare at the empty space he had occupied a second before. Now, when a ghost decides to leave, they'll dematerialize and then end up wherever they want to go. Marler had decided to leave and there would be no calling him back, at least for the present.

To his confused way of thinking, he had more pressing priorities than talking to me. If he had given me the chance, I could have explained to him that the real issue trapping him in the Ghost Realm was not the need to take care of the Cape San Blas Lighthouse, but his subconscious need for redemption. Redemption from the consequences of that fatal, impulsive moment of bad judgment when he became involved with the treacherous Miss Velma Reynolds. One of the consequences was being murdered in his prime, thereby preventing him from looking after his beloved wife and daughters. There had been so much promise for the future for the young family. Then Susie had been left to raise them on her own.

And what about the seamen whose lives he had been responsible for by fulfilling his duty to the job? He had let them down also.

Yes, I could see that to Marler's confused way of thinking, he had a lot to atone for. It was this self-condemnation that prevented him from crossing over to the Other Side. To him, because of his confused mental and emotional state, continuing to take care of the lighthouse was a way to prove that he was a responsible, trustworthy man after all—a man deserving of the love and trust of his family, and of entrance to the Other Side.

"I will earn all of this back, yes I will!" the ghost keeps telling himself over and over. He fails to realize that there's nothing for him to redeem, prove, or earn. The only thing he has to do to change his present wretched state of existence is to move past his regrets and guilt so that he will be able to forgive himself. Then he will allow himself to move on from the cold, sterile existence of the Ghost Realm into the warm, loving Light of the Other Side. How long will it take before Marler, the duty-bound lighthouse ghost, moves on? I can assure you that even he doesn't know.

I always find it rather ironic and sad that Marler and all the other spirits who've imprisoned themselves in the Ghost Realm hold the keys to their freedom (remember free will?) but are the last to allow themselves to use them. Marler demonstrated this by leaving abruptly to continue going about his senseless duties. The ghost was gone by choice, though, so there was nothing further I could do.

Oh well, you can't win 'em all—or rather, *help* them all—unless they choose to help themselves (hmm, sounds kinda like us humans, right?) by letting go of their obsessions! It was time for Beth and me to go.

Before leaving, we went by the gift shop to say goodbye to Beverly and thank her for her hospitality. She greeted us with an amused grin and the question, "Well, did ya run into any ghosts over there?"

"Yes, we did," I answered with a laugh. "The Cape San Blas Lighthouse is haunted!" Still chuckling, I told her, "Just think, Beverly, on those dark nights out here when you think you're by yourself, you're not. Marler's ghost is right there with you, following you around as you two look after the old lighthouse."

Now most people might pause in consternation at the thought that a ghost was following them around on a dark, moonless night. Beverly, however, just laughed and exclaimed, "Glad to have the company! He just better not disturb my sleep!"

I couldn't have agreed more. As we walked out the door, I thought, *That Beverly is one tough lady. I'm sure between her* and Marler the lighthouse ghost, the Cape San Blas Lighthouse is in good hands, human and otherwise!

Haunted Cape San Blas Lighthouse

THE PERMANENT GUESTS OF THE RUMBLE SEAT INN BED AND BREAKFAST

The Rumble Seat Inn Bed and Breakfast, along with its ghostly residents, is located in downtown Barnesville, Georgia. It's a beautiful Victorian mansion built at the end of the nineteenth century. When you look at this beautiful house from the outside, it appears just like any other ordinary old house. But wait, what about the inside of the house? Ordinary? Not!

The mansion has developed a well-earned reputation over the years for being haunted. People walking on the street at night have seen lights blinking on and off throughout the years during the periods the old mansion stood empty of any living inhabitants. These blinking lights shine out brightly, even when the electricity has been turned off. Shadowy figures that no one can explain have been seen walking on the grounds around the house. Local residents also claim there's a creepy feeling to the old house when you get up close to it. So it's no wonder that the old house has stayed vacant over the years more often than not.

At this time, though, the old mansion not only has its ghostly inhabitants, but two intrepid human residents as well: Jenny Dawn Castillo, the owner, and her daughter, Emily.

Of course, the Rumble Seat didn't start off haunted. It was built in 1892 by a Dr. Connally. He died five years later in 1897. Dr. Smith Rumble bought it in 1900 for his bride, Anna. They had six children, but one was stillborn and another died three days after birth.

The good doctor was well respected and had a busy practice in town. He and his wife enjoyed a busy social life. They were a much-sought-after couple on the entertainment scene in thriving Barnesville and the surrounding area. Anna also enjoyed throwing lavish parties at their mansion, where she was the belle of the ball.

Although Anna's origins had been humble and hardscrabble, you would never have known it. She quickly got used to the social life and the servants that went along with being the wife of the successful town doctor. You would think that with Anna's humble origins, she would have had empathy for those less fortunate. Not so; she behaved quite to the contrary. She put on airs and saw herself as superior to anyone not measuring up to her exacting standards of social acceptance. Her social standing was something she worked at constantly to maintain.

Therefore, it was a shock when the good doctor died of stomach cancer in 1913 at the age of fifty-four. The doctor's death left Anna by herself to raise four children, maintain the huge house, and keep the servants paid. Tough times had arrived for the Rumble family. Her attitude of superiority over others through the years had not garnered her many true friends, either. Her diminishing financial situation caused her social standing to go into decline. Because her friendships had been established on the superficial foundation of money, when she ended up broke, the wealthy matrons she had courted as friends no longer called upon her. Now unable to throw lavish parties, she was no longer invited to any.

Yet even when she had had money, Anna hadn't endeared herself to many people because of her private, somewhat defensive personality. The one thing she felt close to and trusted was her mansion. She loved her home. Despite the poverty in her life, Anna was determined to overcome any hardships to keep her mansion, and she proved just as determined to keep it in death. She felt that the impressive house proved who she was, still someone of worth no matter what.

Anna died in 1961 at the age of ninety-one. Her beloved mansion was sold by the Rumble descendants in 1983. Although it was sold to a succession of buyers over the years, none stayed for long. There was something about the drafty, old house that was too creepy to handle. Word spread that the place was haunted. Eventually, the house sat vacant for longer and longer periods.

Then Jenny came along. Jenny is a talented chef who runs her own successful catering business. She saw the big house one day and fell in love with it. When she learned it was for sale, she jumped at the chance to buy it, and thus the Rumble Seat Inn Bed and Breakfast was born.

Having sat unloved for so long, the old house needed renovating right from the start. Jenny, a woman of many talents, lovingly did most of the restoration work herself such as painting, hanging drywall, and furnishing it with period furniture. The Rumble mansion was on the way to being restored to its former grandeur. She told me that, until she started the restoration, she hadn't realized she had bought some extra fixtures that came with the house. Nobody had told Jenny the old house was haunted. It didn't take Jenny long to find out, though. She had ghosts!

She told me that on many nights, when she was working alone in the cavernous house, it felt like something was following her around, watching her. Then there were the footsteps walking along the upstairs hall. She could follow their progress along the hall as she painted the rooms downstairs. Sometimes, whatever it was would stop directly above her and then resume its walking.

Jenny confessed that on many nights she was terrified because of the constant unexplained activity. Despite this fear of what she could feel and hear but not see, she finished the renovation. The Rumble Seat Inn Bed and Breakfast was opened for business.

Miss Anna's pride and joy, the Rumble House, now the Rumble Seat Inn Bed and Breakfast

The Rumble Seat now restored to its former grandeur

From the first day, guests have asked Jenny about the otherworldly activity that takes place at the inn. One question often asked of Jenny is "Why is someone upstairs slamming doors?" This inquiry comes only after the noise gets too loud and constant for the puzzled guest to ignore.

"There's no one upstairs at the moment," Jenny explains to her skeptical listener. They always look at her in disbelief.

Then there are the footsteps heard throughout the house with no body attached to them—at least, no earthly body. One guest even said that somebody kept opening and closing the door to his room, going in and out. "I was kept up all night!" he complained.

"I assure you that at three in the morning, everyone was asleep in this house," Jenny told him.

Then there were the Junior Leaguers who came to the mansion for a tour of historic homes. Jenny was ushering them proudly throughout the house when they reached the parlor. The minute the group stepped into the parlor, the overhead lights started flickering. After a few moments of this activity, the lights went out, leaving the society ladies in the dark. The lights continued to stay on in every other room in the mansion.

After the ladies left, the lights came back on in the parlor. Now, Jenny knew that she'd had the electrical wiring rewired and updated. Nonetheless, she called the electrician to come out and check the wiring in the parlor.

"Ma'am, everything checks out just fine," he assured her.

At this point, Jenny decided enough was enough. She wanted to know what was going on in her house. Her curiosity overcoming her fear, Jenny called me, an old friend, and wanted to know if I'd be willing to come down for a weekend to investigate the strange events going on at the mansion.

"Of course I'd like to come!" I told her. What else would a good friend do except be there for you? Of course, it helps if that good friend, me, happens to like ghosts! It also helps make the adventure more alluring if your hostess for the weekend, Jenny, happens to be an internationally trained chef!

My friend Peggy Stancil agreed to come do the photography for the investigation. She wasn't so sure she liked ghosts, but she is a good friend. We arrived in Barnesville on a rainy Saturday morning. As we drove up to the impressive old mansion to park, I could see an elderly lady, or rather the ghost of an elderly lady, watching us from an upstairs window. At that moment, Jenny came down the steps and greeted us like the gracious hostess she is. She ushered us in and showed us to a spacious upstairs bedroom where we could put our bags and equipment.

We had barely set them down when the elderly lady ghost glided into the room. She didn't say anything at first, but I got the impression she was checking us out to see if we were worthy of her hospitality.

I described her to Jenny.

"What is her name?" she excitedly asked me. I telepathically asked the lady her name.

"Miss Anna," she replied.

When I told Jenny her name, she clapped her hands and exclaimed, "I knew it! I just knew it! I felt her with me when I was working on the house."

Miss Anna, as she liked to be called, said, "I did indeed follow Jenny around to make sure everything was done properly." She had wanted to make sure that Jenny was not going to treat her beloved house the way the previous owner had. He had stripped it of its fine furnishings and let it fall into disrepair.

Jenny wanted to know why the paranormal activity had lessened once the restoration work was finished. Miss Anna explained, "At one time there were a lot more ghosts hanging around the house. I allowed them to stay in exchange for their help in driving away undesirable owners and prospective buyers. I approve of what Jenny is doing with my house, so the other ghosts were no longer needed. I sent them on their way."

Miss Anna when she was young

Miss Anna had never relinquished her title as mistress of the Rumble house. She saw the Rumble Seat Inn Bed and Breakfast as a second chance to have the social life she once had, even if she enjoyed it while being in another form. Once again she could play the popular hostess, which is what she did during our entire visit. She followed us around the house as we investigated, making sure everything went well. Even though Miss Anna played the society hostess for a short time while alive, and was doing so even now, she had not always lived in a grand home, or had money and servants to command. Her early life had been a hardscrabble existence. The one bright spot during this bleak time had been her talent as an artist. "It was the one thing I was able to find pleasure in," she said.

At this point, our talk was interrupted by the arrival of Miss Anna's granddaughter, Mrs. Virginia Legg. Jenny had asked her to participate in this afternoon's proceedings.

Virginia had moved in with her grandmother Anna when she was a little girl of four. She had grown up in the mansion. She would be an invaluable resource to answer any questions about the house and the Rumble family. Virginia was not only a delightful lady, but a talented artist in her own right. She confessed that her family knew little about Anna's early life before she married Dr. Rumble. Anna had refused to talk about it much. At this point, Anna herself joined the conversation, glad for the chance to communicate with her beloved granddaughter.

She told Virginia, "I love you so much. I just wish I had told you and my other loved ones when I was alive and they could hear me. I'm so proud of you with your fine character and great artistic talent. I do believe you inherited your talent from me."

It appeared that Miss Anna was finally ready to open up about the hidden period of her early life. This opening up would hopefully serve as the catharsis she needed to start healing the old wounds from her previous earthly life. Eagerly, she began. "Most of the memories from my childhood were not pleasant ones. My father was a drinking man who turned more and more to the bottle. He was fine when not drinking, but when he was, we children would keep our distance from him. He would lash out at anyone and anything when under the influence.

"Another main cause of my bad memories was the extreme state of poverty my large family lived in. Many nights we children went to bed hungry. Our clothes were always old and threadbare. I remember feeling jealous of other girls and their nice dresses. My family was ostracized because of our poverty, and the fact that we weren't townspeople. Our shack was located on the outskirts of town. I had few friends because I was too embarrassed by my family and our house to ask them over after school.

"The one bright spot in my life that gave me hope was my art. My art made me feel special. My family didn't have the money for me to take lessons, so I taught myself by studying and drawing the pictures in the schoolbooks. I drew on whatever materials I could get my hands on—old pieces of boards, scraps of paper, anything. I was naturally talented, so drawing and painting came easily to me.

"In my teens, I took any odd jobs I could get just to buy canvas and paints. At this point I started drawing and painting in earnest. By my late teens, my art had become my passion. If I were good enough as an artist, I reasoned, it would provide a means for me to escape my life of poverty. I would also be given the respect and approval from others that I had yearned for, but not had, while growing up.

"Meanwhile, my family was doing everything they could to discourage me from pursuing my dream. They ridiculed me for taking this more unconventional path toward making a better life for myself. While other people told me my paintings were beautiful and showed great promise, my family would criticize them.

" 'Find a good man,' they would say. 'Your art will never support you. You're not good enough.'

"Finally, I stopped showing them any of my work. The only family member who believed in me and my talent was my aunt. One day she came to me and asked if I would like to take my paintings to a dealer she had heard about in New York City. She said she would accompany me and pay for the trip. My uncle would come along as chaperone. So, off I went to the big city with all of my hopes and dreams wrapped up in my paintings."

At this point, Anna clairvoyantly showed me herself as a young Anna. She and her aunt were crossing a busy street in turn-of-the-nineteenth-century New York. Their long gowns swept the dusty road as they walked toward a row of brownstone buildings with broad steps leading up to each one. Anna was carrying some of her best paintings under her arm as she proudly strode toward her bright future. She would show everyone back home who had ever doubted her talent that they were wrong!

A half hour later, Anna and her aunt came out of the dealer's gallery. Tears were streaming down her face as she stumbled down the steps. She looked absolutely crushed. "He told me I was a talentless hack! He also said, 'Women have no business being professional artists,' that it was improper. He barely looked at my paintings. He told me, 'A woman's place is in the home, not in an art gallery.' "

At this point, my guides interjected that Anna had indeed been talented and her paintings quite good. The art dealer had been laboring under a commonly held misconception of the time about what women were capable of and what their proper role in society was. He had sent Anna away with a last admonishment: to go home, find a good husband, and make sure she pleased him as a helpmate. Anna did just that.

"The first thing I did when I returned home was to go to the backyard, build a fire, and burn all of my paintings one after the other. I burned every last one! I vowed never to pick up my paints and brushes again. I threw them all away. I wanted no reminders of my failure and shame. My family understood that I never wanted to talk about my art again. From that time on, it was never mentioned."

At this point in Anna's narrative, Virginia excitedly interjected with, "There have been rumors in the family throughout the years that Grandmother Anna had been a talented artist. It was always a mystery, though. If she really were, then where were the paintings? Not a one has ever turned up."

Anna herself had never confirmed nor denied the allegations. She just refused to discuss her life before marriage, period. After she had closed the door—or rather, slammed it shut—on this earlier period of her life, she chose an easier way to escape what she perceived as her low station in life. "I now set about the business, like every other young woman my age, of finding myself a suitable husband. I was eventually introduced to Dr. Smith Rumble. He was taken with me, if I do say so myself. He courted me, we got married, and I settled down to being a good wife. It was as simple as that. I respected him at first, but learned to love him later. You know the rest of my story," Anna said.

She then directly addressed her granddaughter, with me acting as the go-between. "Know this, Virginia. With your artistic talent, you can go far. You're a chip off the old block—me. Don't do as I did with my life, though, and let someone else tell you who you're going to be. To allow this is to give up on your dreams, who you are."

With this advice, Miss Anna leaned over and gave her beloved granddaughter a hug. She kissed the top of Virginia's head, and with a last "I love you" glided out of the room. Then, ever the proper lady, she peeped back in. "Thank you, Miss Boo."

After Miss Anna's narrative, it was obvious that she had allowed the negative events in her life to make her bitter. Instead of taking control over the events and channeling them into something positive for her life, she had repeatedly played the role of victim. When she died an elderly, bitter woman, she had chosen to stay with her beloved house instead of moving on to the Other Side. Staying in the house was the one thing that made her feel like she was someone special. In life she had allowed, and encouraged, others to define who she was by the material things around her. This obsessive attachment to a material object—the house—that could be used to superficially define her as worthy was what had caused her to become trapped in it as a ghost.

She was a being trapped between the realm of the living and the realm of Spirit. So once again, but this time in death, Anna had chosen to not live fully but just to exist.

Yet, I did have hope for her finding peace, for she had told me earlier when I had asked her about crossing over to the Other Side that "I will move on once I see that Miss Jenny can look after my house properly." She had also admitted that she was once again enjoying playing hostess, even if it was in a different form. With a mischievous grin and a chuckle, she had told me, "At least now I don't have to worry about my gowns being in the latest fashion!"

I thought, *How nice it is to find a ghost who still has a sense of humor despite the sadness of its trapped, ghostly existence.*

After Miss Anna's departure, Virginia said that she must be leaving also. We saw her to the door and then returned to take photos. Later, we sat down to one of Jenny's delicious gourmet dinners. Far more experienced food critics than Peggy and I have raved about Jenny's culinary skills.

After dinner, it was time for Peggy and I to continue investigating the mansion. An apprehensive yet curious Jenny and her two daughters, Emily and Allie, accompanied us. Emily and Allie are two delightful, lively young women. Both confessed that most of the time in the house, they were terrified. Usually Allie was away at college. Emily, on the other hand, was a high school senior living at home. She admitted that on many nights she would sleep in her mother's room when the ghostly activity in her own room became too disturbing.

And so, with trepidation showing on their faces, Jenny and the two girls followed us into the kitchen. Although it's been modernized to accommodate Jenny's catering business, it's still basically like it was when the house was built at the turn of the nineteenth century. As I walked around the kitchen, I felt drawn to the large pantry located in the far corner. There, peaking out of the doorway, was a small, dark-haired little boy of four or five. He had blue eyes and was dressed in short pants and stockings, typical children's clothes from the early 1900s. It was obvious from the quality of the clothes he wore that he had been a child from a privileged background.

At the moment, though, he was looking rather lost as he sucked on his thumb. I went over and knelt down in front of him. Small ghost children are the same as small human children; they can feel rather intimidated by someone towering over them. Therefore, I always kneel when talking to them to gain their trust. "What is your name?" I asked him.

He hesitated for a moment before answering, "Robert."

"What are you doing here, Robert?"

"I'm looking for the doctor."

"Why are you looking for the doctor?"

"So he can make me better, and I can go home to Mama and Daddy." At the mention of his parents, tears of sadness and fear trickled down his small, thin face.

"What happened to you?" I asked gently. "How did you die?"

"Don't know" was his simple answer. Because of his young age, he didn't understand that he had passed from the earthly realm. He had no concept of death for the human body. He was existing in his own time period as if he were still alive. Needing to get answers but not wanting to upset him any more than he already was, I patiently asked, "Why are you here in Jenny's kitchen?"

"Because she's Doctor's cook. But she don't pay me any attention."

"That's right," interjected Miss Anna, who had been following us around. "Children should be seen, not heard, and that's 'doesn't,' not 'don't'!"

Always the proper lady, I thought with amusement.

Robert thought otherwise. With tears in his eyes, he answered her with, "I'm a good boy, I am. I'm a good boy!"

From what he had said about Jenny, he thought she was one of Dr. Rumble's house servants. Even as we were talking, he went over to Jenny's right side while she was standing at the sink. He reached up and pulled on her apron. "Where's Doctor? Where's Doctor?" he pleaded. When she didn't answer (only because she couldn't see and hear that he was there), he left to go walk through the house to look for Dr. Rumble himself. Dr. Rumble had passed long ago. Robert didn't realize this, though.

From what I could piece together from his confused, five-year-old's state of mind, he had felt sick and hot one day. His mother took him to Dr. Rumble's house to get some medicine. When he and his mother got back home, Robert was put to bed. He progressively got worse, though, first burning up with fever and then freezing with cold. Toward the end, he became dizzy and disoriented. The last thing he heard and remembered before he died was his mother screaming, "Get the doctor! For God's sake, get the doctor!"

When he "woke up," he was aware of his mama and daddy crying and sobbing by his bedside. He talked to them, but they ignored him. Robert knew something was wrong, but he didn't know what. He tried to stay close to his family to find out what was happening, but the all-pervading energy of sadness and grief that filled the house frightened and upset him.

And so it was that, unbeknownst to Dr. Rumble, he had a small spirit accompany him home after he finished examining the little boy's body. To Robert's way of thinking, didn't his mama call for the doctor at the last to help? This doctor would have the answers. The problem was that Dr. Rumble couldn't see the little ghost that had latched on to him, so he unintentionally ignored Robert's pleas for help.

When they reached the Rumble house, it was habit that caused Robert to go to the kitchen. He had been unable to get the doctor's attention. To him, this was the same way he had been treated by his own family when alive. Everyone in his wealthy, busy family had been too preoccupied to pay much attention to him. Therefore, he always ended up talking to the family cook to get attention. She was always kind to Robert, making time for him whenever he came to visit. Cook always had a treat from the pantry waiting for him. He now called Jenny "Cook," just like what he always called his family's cook.

As I finished telling Robert's story, he showed back up, walking through the kitchen wall to rejoin us. He looked dejected from his fruitless search for the doctor. I explained to him that he had died years ago, and that Dr. Rumble himself had also passed long ago. The doctor was no longer here to help Robert. "Would you like to move on, go into the Light?" I asked him.

"No!" he stated without hesitation. It seemed as if Robert was content to keep Jenny company in the kitchen. I asked Jenny if it was okay if the little boy ghost stayed with her.

"No problem," she tenderly assured him. Jenny is the type of person who loves children and animals, regardless of the form they come in. Robert chimed in with the request that Jenny talk to him more. "I would love to, Robert," she responded kindly.

It was time to leave Robert and continue our exploration of the mansion. Before we left, I explained to him that when the time came that he wanted to go into the Light of the Divine to see his mama and daddy, all he had to do was call upon an angel. With his assurance that he understood, we left the kitchen, leaving one delightful little ghost playing in the pantry.

The next area of the house we went to was the upstairs section. As we walked along the hall toward the bedroom at the end, the energy started to feel oppressive. This bedroom is called the Virginia Room. Jenny named it for Miss Anna's granddaughter Virginia, who had slept in it as a little girl. Jenny told me later that Virginia confessed she had always been terrified of the room. It was always freezing cold, and she never felt like she was alone in it. Someone—or something—always seemed to be watching her.

When I entered the room, I immediately saw the ghost of a young man sitting on the bed. He appeared to be around eighteen or nineteen years old. The ghost had a sickly, confused energy about him. What riveted my attention, though, was the horrible-looking wound on his right leg. The leg had been badly burned from midthigh all the way down to midcalf. The area was also covered with red, raw-looking sores where it had never completely healed.

I went over and sat next to him on the bed. He watched me, wondering what I was up to. There was a deep sorrow around this young man that permeated the room, giving it a heavy energy. "What is your name?" I asked him.

After a moment of sizing me up, he answered, "Ancil."

"Why are you here in the Rumble house?"

"Because Miss Anna lets me stay," he answered shortly. This ghost was definitely not the chatty type. Because of his obvious unwillingness to communicate, I decided to get right to the point before he decided not to talk to me at all. After all, it would be his choice, not mine, if he decided to do so or not.

"What happened to you? Why do you want to stay?"

"Because I can't go home anymore. I did something terrible and I'm afraid to face my family." Ancil now paused, reticent to say anymore. The shame he was feeling that caused this reticence was palpable all around him. He turned away, and for a moment I thought he wasn't going to say anymore. I continued to sit patiently next to him, though, calmly talking all the while. With this gentle encouragement, he turned back to me and started telling his story.

"In 1916, I was called to serve my country as a soldier in World War I. My family, especially my father, was very proud of me. Up until that time, I never felt like he approved of me. No matter how hard I tried, it was never good enough. But now I was a hero and was treated as such whenever I came home. Life was going swell. Then, in the winter of 1917, I was placed on the front lines in a battle with the Huns. I was running across the battlefield when the man next to me screamed, 'Gas! Gas!'

"At that moment I remember stepping down into a puddle of oily liquid. I ran a few more feet and fell. My right leg felt like it was on fire. The last thing I remember before I blacked out was rolling on the ground, screaming in pain.

"When I came to, I was in a field hospital. I overheard the doctor telling the nurse it was a shame I hadn't been brought in sooner so the damage wouldn't have been so great. Because of the prolonged exposure to the mustard gas, there was extensive nerve and tissue damage up and down my right leg. I stayed in the hospital for months, where they kept me on morphine for the constant pain. I wasn't healing properly, though, so I was ruled unfit for duty and sent home.

"I still needed to be under a doctor's care, so the logical choice was the doctor who replaced Dr. Rumble a few years ago after his death. Dr. Rumble had not only been the family doctor, but also a family friend. My parents had trusted Dr. Rumble because he was a fine, caring doctor. The man who took over his practice was not nearly as good, or caring. My parents had no way of knowing this, though. The new doctor preferred to keep me on morphine instead of finding other treatments.

"Over time, the tissues on my leg drew up tightly, impeding my ability to walk. I had to walk with a cane. As time went on, I became a bitter, drug-addicted derelict in my hometown, making me a disgrace to my family. I know this because my father told me often enough what a disgrace I was as a man. 'Only a weakling would whine about some pain and become a drug addict!' he would angrily tell me. I knew his anger came from embarrassment of me. I didn't blame him . . . I was embarrassed about myself also.

"One day I decided I had had enough of the pain and misery my life had become. I went into some woods outside of town, took an overdose of morphine, and lay down to die. It was as simple as that. When I woke up, though, I wanted to change my mind. But as I stood outside of my unmoving, physical body, looking down on it, I realized it was dead. I could not get back into it. There was no going back. It was too late.

"My decision had been made while in a confused mental and emotional state from the pain and drug addiction. Looking around, I felt so scared and alone. I didn't know where to go. I could never go home again. I was not brave enough to face my father's anger and disappointment over what I had done, for I would surely hear him call me a coward once again."

My guides told me that Ancil was mistaken about this. The truth was that his father had been filled with regret and anguish until the day he died because of how he had treated his son. My guides also told me that Ancil had been in the midst of learning one of his great life lessons when he cut it short by committing suicide. The lesson had been to learn to love himself as unconditionally as possible, regardless of what mistakes he had made in the past. If he had been able to do this, he would have understood before it was too late that these mistakes were merely opportunities for him to learn and grow in life. That there was, given time and love, always the possibility to change these "mistakes" for the better. Another part of this lesson was to love himself enough so that he didn't let others' judgments of him influence how he felt about himself.

But now he had no life at all. By ending it, he had given up the chance to change things. Ancil, who was listening closely to this communication between my guides and myself, nodded in understanding.

"Where did you go after you ended your own life?" I asked him.

"I came here to the Rumble house because Dr. Rumble had always treated me kindly. He never judged me. When Miss Anna died, she found me here. She told me I could stay if I helped her look after the house by protecting it from interlopers."

"Do you ever think about crossing over to the Other Side?"

"Yes," he said, "but I'm not ready to face my parents' hurt yet over what I did. I don't want to see my father. I'd rather stay here and help Miss Anna and Miss Jenny run the house, if it's okay with Miss Jenny."

I told Jenny of Ancil's request.

"Of course it's okay for him to stay," she replied. "As long as he behaves himself, he'll be welcome."

We told Ancil goodbye and then moved on to check out Emily's room. There, huddled in the far corner, was the ghost of a teenage girl. Her head was bowed with her hands up in front of her face. Although I couldn't see her countenance clearly, she appeared to be crying. When she lifted her head to look at us, her long hair fell back from her face. There was blood all over it. There was also a lot of blood down the front of her clothes. Her head was cocked at an odd angle, as if her neck was broken.

She was obviously distraught over something. Talking quietly, wanting to give her time to get used to my presence, I introduced myself. "Hi, my name is Boo. Would you mind if I talked to you for a while?"

She assented with a simple "Okay."

"How'd you die?" I asked her.

Dashing the tears away with the back of a bloodstained hand, she said, "I was not supposed to be with my boyfriend that night. I snuck out to be with him. He was drinking when he picked me up in his car. When I saw the liquor bottle, I didn't want to go. I almost didn't get in the car, but I didn't want him to think I wasn't cool enough to be with him, so I got in. We were driving along, laughing and drinking. He was going fast like he always did. All of a sudden, something smashed into us! We were in a terrible car accident. That's the last thing I remember until I woke up and saw my body on the road with people working over it."

From her clothes, it looked like she had been killed in the early sixties, and I said as much. She confirmed with a simple nod of her head. Now usually it's a silent, telepathic conversation between myself and the ghost, but when the living are present as they were right then, I verbalize the whole conversation as it takes place between the ghost and I. In this way, the living will get the whole story, even if they can't hear the ghost's half of it.

While repeating the conversation as the ghost and I spoke, Emily nudged Allie with her elbow. They both bolted out of the room and flew down the stairs. They weren't gone more than a few minutes when they came running back up the stairs, screaming, "Oh my God, she's real, she's real! We looked her up on the computer and it said she was killed in a bad car accident in 1963!"

Both girls looked stunned and uncomfortable with what they had discovered, but I couldn't help but be amused by their reaction. I know that everyone will eventually have the epiphany from some otherworldly contact that ghosts and the Ghost Realm do exist. After all, there are thousands of realms of existence out there besides ours! How boring it would be if we humans were the only ones around.

Getting things back on track after Emily and Allie's excited announcement, I asked the teenage ghost, "Why are you still here hanging out at the Rumble Seat?"

"I can't go home yet," she said. "My parents are too upset over my death. My daddy acts mad and Mama cries all the time. It's too upsetting for me, for all of us. When alive, I would come over to the Rumble house to visit some of the kids. I figured it'd be a good place to hang out till things calm down at home. Then I'll pay Mama and Daddy a visit and say goodbye."

It was obvious that this young ghost girl, although she knew she was dead, was unaware of the passage of time.

The reason for this cluelessness and confusion on the part of ghosts is that there's no linear time in the Spirit Realm as we know it in the Earth Realm. They have no idea as to how much time has passed them by.

Such was the case with this teenage ghost. She thought it was only yesterday that she had been killed. In fact, fifty years had passed since her fatal accident.

Interrupting my thoughts with a giggle, she stated, "It's not so bad hanging out here for now. I like Emily's room the best. It's got good vibes and the music is groovy! I especially like to hang out with her friends when they come up to the room to visit."

The teenage ghost showed me how she would sit on the bed among Emily's friends as they talked. I could see it now, a group of typical teenage girls laughing and gossiping, and one atypical teenager avidly listening. Obviously, Emily could also visualize it, for she turned pale at the realization that not all of her visiting friends were from her world.

At the end of her narrative, the ghost got up to leave. "Emily, let me know when our friends are coming over. I'll be waiting!"

Emily didn't know what to say, so she simply said nothing. I, on the other hand, knew I needed to say a few more things to the teenage ghost before she left us. "Are you aware of the passage of time, how long you've been in the Ghost Realm?" I asked.

"What do you mean?"

I explained the passage of physical, earthly time, and how long she had been a ghost. She was astonished. I then asked her if she was ready to cross over to the Other Side, Heaven.

"No, not yet!" she quickly answered. "I want to hang out with Emily and my other friends a while longer."

I could tell she wasn't ready to cross, and this was her decision to make, not mine. I did tell her, though, that she could move on any time she liked.

"How?" she asked.

"When you get ready, call upon an angel to come to you. The angel will arrange your trip Home to the Other Side."

With a slight smile she nodded in understanding, turned away once again, and walked through the wall, headed for some other part of the house.

It was now late, so everyone decided to call it a day. Jenny let Peggy have her bedroom because of the beautiful antique tub it possessed. Peggy couldn't wait to try it out. As we left her in the bedroom preparing to bathe, I couldn't help but laugh, though, because of the ghostly, leering faces peeking around the door from the antechamber. From the lecherous looks on their faces, they couldn't wait for her to try it out either!

Hearing me laugh, Peggy asked, "What are you laughing at, Boo?"

"Oh nothing, Peggy," I stated with my best innocent face. For who am I to spoil the ghosts' fun? These ghosts were minor characters who came and went in the mansion. Even though they were harmless, they looked positively degenerate!

Jenny was going to sleep in the Virginia Room—rather apprehensively, I might add, for she knew the disturbed, unstable Ancil awaited her there. I myself would sleep in the Rumble Suite. This had been Smith and Anna's room.

When I walked in, I could smell Miss Anna's old-fashioned perfume. She had been here to make sure of the comfort of her guest. I settled in for the night, knowing that we would be up early the next morning to compare notes on any happenings from the night before.

Yet if anything happened in my room during the night, I was unaware of it. Early the next morning, however, I was awakened by the smell of Miss Anna's perfume as she approached the bed. The scent grew stronger and stronger as she drew closer. Now I'm not one to be very talkative early in the morning, be it with a ghost or human, so I kept my eyes closed, pretending to sleep. I could sense her standing over me though, wanting to talk.

Realizing that she was not going to go away because of her hostess concern for me, I opened my eyes. "Good morning, Miss Anna. How are you?"

"Fine, dear. How did you sleep?"

"Like a log," I replied.

"Oh good, I was hoping so. I made sure the other ghosts didn't disturb you during the night. I gave strict orders that they were not to come in here while you slept."

"Thank you, Miss Anna. You run a tight, orderly household," I complimented.

"Thank you, my dear. I do the best I can with what I have to work with," she said. I wondered if she were talking about her lack of funds when she was alive or the beings she now existed with in death. Ghosts can be a lively, hard lot to manage!

Just then Jenny knocked and came in to tell me that breakfast was ready. She must have known that I always wake up hungry and ready to eat. Before heading to breakfast, I checked the recorder I had placed by the bedside table the previous night. Sure enough, it had picked up Miss Anna's light footsteps as she walked around the room, making sure everything was in order. There was also the sound of water running in the tub in the antechamber. Had the solicitous Miss Anna been drawing a morning bath for me, albeit a ghostly one?

When I went into the mansion's charming living room, Jenny had a cozy fire going and a beautiful breakfast laid out for us. Nobody could ever accuse Jenny of not taking the best care of her guests. She and Miss Anna made a good team.

In walked Peggy looking rather tired and disheveled. I asked her how her night had gone.

"Okay," she stated, "but about four o'clock I was awakened by something walking up and down the hall. Then I heard a rapid thumping sound outside my door, like someone was playing a snare drum."

"How did your bath go last night?" I innocently asked her.

I could barely contain my laughter when Peggy blushed a bright red. "I enjoyed the bath, but it was hard to stay warm despite the hot water temperature! There were cold spots and breezes around me and then they would disappear. I never was able to stay warm in the bath. I also felt uncomfortable and had a hard time relaxing. It was like I was being watched while naked by a whole crowd of people!"

I couldn't hold my laughter any longer. "You did indeed have a whole crowd joining you for your bath, Peggy. Your bathing companions were ghosts, though, and not a hunk in the bunch!"

She also complained of having some rather shocking, lascivious, and unpleasant thoughts while in the bath. "I felt like they weren't my thoughts at all," she stated. Knowing Peggy for the proper lady she is, I knew this to be true. Even now she was blushing again as she told us about her bathing experience.

I told her that under the right emotional or physical conditions, ghosts are able to implant thoughts in a person's mind. They can also influence a person's actions if that person is susceptible in the first place. If the person isn't, they can't. One example is an alcoholic. They might attract a ghost who had a drinking problem while alive. Still wanting that alcoholic high even in death, the only way for the ghost to experience it would be through inhabitation of a borrowed human body. Therefore, to keep the liquor flowing, they'll try to influence and maintain the alcoholic's continued addiction.

"Okay, I understand how ghosts can influence people, but what about the footsteps walking back and forth in the hall that woke me up early this morning?" she asked.

Jenny told her that quite a few guests ask her about the person stomping around the hallways in the morning. They say that when they open the door to look out to see who is walking around, the footsteps stop. Much to their surprise, there is no one in the hall—at least no one they can see.

Now it was Jenny's turn. We asked her how she had fared in the Virginia Room. "Not too well," she stated with a tired sigh. Out of all the rooms in her haunted mansion, this is the only room she doesn't like. The night before it had taken her a long time to relax enough to fall asleep.

"Something kept playing with the hair on the top of my head," she explained. "As if that weren't bad enough, I would then feel the hands go to my feet. Then they would work their way up my body, pressing down on me as they went. When the hands started playing in my hair for the umpteenth time, I decided I had been frightened long enough.

"'Ancil!' I said in no uncertain terms. 'I've had enough! Please leave me alone and don't bother me anymore tonight.' He gently pulled my hair one last time and then acquiesced. I was not disturbed anymore."

One could hardly blame Jenny for the relief that was evident in her voice as she said this. Ghosts don't need sleep; human bodies do.

I told them about the perfume smell in my room. Jenny said that many guests had asked her about this, stating that it reminded them of their grandmother's perfume.

So, from the many observations of the numerous guests who have stayed at the Rumble Seat Inn Bed and Breakfast, it's obvious that Jenny's beloved mansion is indeed haunted. In her usual calm, lighthearted way, Jenny takes all of this ghostly activity in stride, always aiming to make sure her guests—both human and otherworldly—feel at home.

Of course, it's obvious she does receive some help carrying out this mission. "Who?" you might ask. Why, the inimitable Miss Anna, of course, standing right there by Jenny's side. So, when arriving at the Rumble Seat Inn Bed and Breakfast, take your pick as to which room you want to bed down in. Be careful which one you choose, though, or you might be sleeping with something more than you bargained for!

THE WOOLFOLK MASSACRE GHOSTS OF ROSE HILL CEMETERY

Macon, the central Georgia city where Rose Hill Cemetery is located, was founded in 1823. Before its founding, though, this area was controlled by the Creek Indians, or Muskogee, as they call themselves. In the late 1700s, settlers came into this area and discovered the wealth of the land. Scattered farms sprang up throughout the Creek territory.

Fort Hawkins was established around 1805 to protect the ever-increasing flow of settlers streaming into the area. The presence of the fort and the growing encroachment by settlers pushed the Creek Nation westward, leaving the area open for further settlement. A community of homesteads, plantations, and commercial ventures was established around the fort. It was at this time that Macon was founded across from the fort on the opposite bank of the Ocmulgee River. Its economy was based on agriculture.

The need for a means of transportation to deliver these agricultural goods brought the railroads into the area. By the latter half of the nineteenth century, Macon had become a major transportation hub. Goods coming in from the agricultural heartland of Georgia had to first go through

Macon before being shipped elsewhere. The rural village transformed into a major city of Georgia. Because of this rapid growth, early Macon became crowded, not only with the living but also the dead. Its two original cemeteries bulged with buried bodies.

Rose Hill Cemetery was founded in 1840 to handle the overflow. It was located on sixty-five acres along the banks of the Ocmulgee River. The new cemetery was named in honor of Simri Rose, the main driving force behind establishing the cemetery. He was also the individual chosen to plan and design the cemetery's layout and landscaping.

Anyone visiting Rose Hill can see the evidence everywhere that Mr. Rose took the committee's trust seriously. His vision and intent was to design it after the garden-type cemeteries found in his native Connecticut. It's like a huge garden, the only difference being that it's a garden shared with the dead. Rose Hill is such a beautiful and peaceful place that the living come even if they're not visiting deceased loved ones. They come for family picnics, get-togethers with friends, or by themselves to take advantage of the peace found in its solitude.

The cemetery is one of the city's oldest and largest burial grounds. It not only holds the remains of thousands of citizens, but also the remains of over six hundred Confederate soldiers. Famous Georgia statesmen and politicians are buried here as well. Rose Hill is also the final resting place for several notable entertainers, such as Duane Allman, his brother Greg, and Berry Oakley of the Allman Brothers Band.

Aside from its celebrities and soldiers, Rose Hill has received its share of victims of tragic deaths. The most well known of these involved members of the Woolfolk family. Nine family members were laid to rest in the Woolfolk family plot on the same day. They had all been brutally slain by another family member, Thomas Woolfolk.

The Woolfolk family plot at Rose Hill Cemetery

Tom was the son of Richard and Susan Woolfolk. Susan, Richard's first wife, had died after Tom's birth on June 18, 1860. Tom's birth had been a difficult ordeal for her, and she had been unable to recover from it. Tom's parents had been very much in love. Richard was so grief stricken over the death of his young wife that he didn't feel capable of taking care of Tom's two older sisters and baby Tom. He decided to send them away from the only home they had known, the family cotton plantation outside of Macon, Georgia.

They went to live with their maternal aunt, Fannie, who lived in Athens, Georgia.

Although Richard's grief was the accepted reason for sending the children away, the real reason was guilt. Susan had never had a hardy constitution, and the two earlier pregnancies had weakened her health further. As a result, the doctor had warned Richard about the danger to Susan if she were to get pregnant again.

But Richard felt he needed a son to pass the plantation on to. Therefore, when Susan did get pregnant with his son and died from the birth, he was unable, or unwilling, to deal with his guilt. To avoid taking responsibility, he transferred the blame to the innocent baby and sent him away. Richard simply didn't want the perceived cause of his grief and guilt, baby Tom, crawling around on the floor as a constant reminder of the fatal pregnancy.

During his formative years, Tom must have become aware of how his father felt about him, and why. The degree to which this knowledge affected his developing psyche would not manifest until many years later, though.

Tom lived with his Aunt Fannie from shortly after his birth till age seven. She doted on the little boy, trying to make up for the loss of his mother and scarcity of love from his father. It was a nurturing environment for Tom, and a great love and fondness developed between him and his aunt.

His idyllic childhood came to an end, though, when his father took a second wife in 1866. In 1867, Richard and Mattie, Tom's new stepmother, decided it was time for him to return to the family farm. It was a case of economics. The more family members, especially male, the more free labor available for the family business of farming. So once again he was torn away from the people who meant the world to him—his beloved sisters and Aunt Fannie.

As a young child, Tom had earned a reputation for being temperamental and high strung. His aunt's loving care had been a stabilizing influence in his life, though, easing his fears and providing an anchor for his emotional, fragile state of mind.

When he was forcibly taken out of this secure relationship, it exacerbated his paranoiac tendencies. Whether it was true or not, he felt that he was moving into a hostile, alien environment. The boy's fears seemed to be validated because when he did rejoin his father, Richard was already invested in Mattie and the family they were starting. Mattie was pregnant at the time of his arrival with Tom's half-brother, Richard Junior.

Tom, used to being the center of doting attention, now found himself pushed aside and ignored. Being moody, defensive, and irritable didn't make it any easier for him to fit in. He resented his stepmother from the start because he blamed her for separating him from his beloved aunt.

Tom's resentment toward her increased as all the attention on the plantation became more and more focused on Mattie and the imminent birth of her first child. With Richard Junior's birth, Richard Senior no longer felt a strong need to establish a rapport with his firstborn son, Tom. He now had not one male heir but two, with more to follow. Mattie proved to be healthier and luckier than Tom's mother when it came to giving birth. She gave Richard Senior six children.

From the start, Tom disliked his stepmother intensely, and they frequently clashed. He blamed her for coming between him and his father. He had little use for his half-siblings either, claiming they treated him like an outsider. He also declared to others that his father's second family was trying to come between him and his rightful inheritance.

Tom was always short of money and unable to succeed at any business venture he tried. Jobs came and went. Therefore, according to everyone, he always seemed to have his eye on his father's properties. He was counting on them to bring him the success that always eluded him.

He even went so far as to ask several people what would happen to the properties if his father died. Who got it, he or his stepmother? Whenever he was told that if his stepmother was alive, she would inherit instead of him, he would go into a rant.

So his family had two big strikes against them in his eyes. They treated him like an outsider, and they were trying to take his inheritance away.

The truth was that a lot of these beliefs were delusions on Tom's part. They originated from his growing mental instability and the resulting paranoia. Whatever the origin of these beliefs was, though, it was a fact to all that, by the time he was grown, Tom passionately hated his stepmother and despised his half-brothers and sisters.

With adulthood came full-blown paranoia. Because of the increasing incidences of bizarre and irrational behavior, the community called him crazy. This mental derangement made it impossible for him to maintain a normal, healthy relationship with anyone for any length of time. He married a young woman named Georgia Bird, but she left him within three weeks. At the time of the divorce, she stated, "He is the meanest man I ever saw, and there's nothing too mean for him to do!"

By his early twenties, Tom's bizarre and paranoiac behavior increased to the point that he was irrationally suspicious of everyone he encountered. No one was immune from his unstable psyche. With no apparent cause or warning, he would start ranting and raving incoherently. When in these rages, he would walk back and forth, waving and pointing the pistol he always kept on his person. People were never sure if he kept it loaded or not until one day, during one of his rages, he pointed it at the ceiling and pulled the trigger. It blew a hole in the plaster.

By August 1887, when he was twenty-seven years old, Tom's bouts of insanity had begun to rapidly increase in frequency. It was at this time that the relationship issues between him and his family came to a horrific climax.

On the early morning of August 6, 1887, between the hours of two and four o'clock, the Woolfolk family was brutally murdered at their plantation, located ten miles outside of Macon. Out of the ten family members residing at the home, Tom was the only one to escape their horrible fate. They had been slaughtered with axes.

The slain family members were Richard Senior and Mattie Woolfolk, ages fifty-four and forty- one, and their six children, Richard Junior, twenty; Pearl, seventeen; Annie, ten; Rosebud, seven; Charlie, five; and Mattie the baby, who was eighteen months old. The ninth victim was Mrs. Temperance West, eighty-four years old. She had come to the Woolfolk plantation from her home in Americas, Georgia, for a visit with her niece Mattie. She was only supposed to stay for a few days. Who knew she would never leave!

Richard and Mattie's family was a close-knit one. On the night of August 5, with all the children around, it was a chaotic scene of laughter and busyness in the old farmhouse.

Tom, who also lived with his parents, was the one exception that night to those enjoying this time of family happiness. He was his usual hostile, paranoid self, resentful of all of them for their closeness. This resentment had been percolating inside him for years. On this night, it would reach its boiling point.

The family went to bed that night, not suspecting the horrible fate that awaited them only hours later. Sleeping peacefully in their beds, they were unaware of the horror creeping toward them in the night. The source of this impending horror was wide awake, though, and working himself up into a killing rage.

Before this night sometime in the recent past, Tom had made the acquaintance of one of the sharecroppers who worked on the Woolfolk farm. The man was a brute with not a shred of conscience to burden him. He had given Richard Senior trouble in the past with his outlaw behavior toward others on the farm. He had a well-earned reputation for being a terrorizing, ruthless bully. Despite the difference between their social positions, Tom had taken up with him because of the one thing they shared—their mutual hatred of the Woolfolk family.

On the night of August 5, unbeknownst to Tom's family, this man came to visit him. He quickly noticed Tom's agitated, emotional state. Taking advantage of this, he stoked the fires of the younger man's mental instability. He kept pushing and haranguing Tom. Tom's rage finally reached the boiling point. The two parted ways after agreeing they would meet later, because now was the time to settle their grudges against Tom's family.

When everyone went to bed later that night, the sharecropper met Tom by the back door. The two entered the house armed with axes. What had they planned to do? Was it going to be merely a robbery, or had they planned something much more sinister for the sleeping family? Nobody knows, nor will they ever.

Whatever their motive, their impulsive plan quickly went awry. For as they moved through the house, Tom started his insane ranting again. His loud ranting woke up Charlie, his five-year-old half-brother. Scared, little Charlie woke up his big brother, Richard Junior, whom he shared a bedroom with. Both boys tried to sneak to their parents' bedroom to awaken their father.

On the way, they caught sight of Tom and his partner in crime. Petrified at the sight of the axes, Richard Junior and Charlie broke into a run for their parents' room in an attempt to get help.

Their panicked movements drew Tom's attention, who looked over and saw them. Realizing that if the two boys reached their parents it would thwart their plan, the two men took off in hot pursuit. The killers rapidly gained on the brothers because little Charlie, with his shorter legs, was having a hard time keeping up with his older brother.

The killers were so close behind, in fact, that the two boys had just managed to run into their parents' room when Tom and his partner caught up with them. By now Tom was in an insane, killing rage. His partner, on the other hand, was deadly calm, for he was a stone-cold killer to whom murder came naturally.

Both men attacked Richard Junior and Charlie with their axes, killing them quickly. The two boys had been helpless against the brutal attack. Their unsuspecting parents fared no better. Not quite awake and still groggy from sleep, they were unable to react swiftly enough when Tom and his partner turned their attention from their dead sons on the floor to them. Wasting no time, the two killers jumped upon the couple as they lay in bed. Richard and Mattie found themselves helpless against Tom and his accomplice's onslaught as they hacked at them again and again with their axes.

Now finished, the killers were turning to leave the death room when they heard a baby crying. There, sitting up in her crib in the corner, was little Mattie, crying and staring around wide eyed. She was the couple's eighteen-month-old toddler. She had gone unnoticed by the killers until the screams of her dying mother and father woke her.

Now the sounds of her frightened crying filled the room. Tom's partner, with not a shred of remorse or hesitation, strode over and silenced her crying with one stroke of his axe.

The two men now turned and headed out of the room without a backward glance at its victims and blood-spattered walls. Running down the hall, they relentlessly moved toward their next helpless prey. On the way to his sisters' bedroom, Tom and his fellow murderer passed the guest bedroom where eighty-four-year-old Temperance West was sleeping. Tom remembered the elderly woman. She was not to be overlooked.

While the other man ran on to his sisters' bedroom, Tom stopped, opened the door, and crept in. He found the elderly lady still sleeping in her bed. Because of a hearing impairment, she had been undisturbed by the blood-curdling screams emanating from the unfolding horror around her. Maybe it was a blessing that she never woke up to the sight of Tom standing over her, eyes glaring viciously with insanity, axe blade upraised, preparing to strike down upon her head twice.

The remaining victims, Tom's half-sisters, were not to be so blessed. They had been awakened by the sounds of struggle and slaughter coming from their parents' room. Waking up confused, they realized too late the true cause for alarm. As had happened with the other victims, they were caught by surprise and so were helpless against the horror that ran into their room.

Even as Tom was killing Temperance, he could hear the screams coming from his sisters' bedroom as his partner brutally attacked them. He ran into the room just in time to see his fellow killer chasing down ten-year-old Annie. She screamed in terror as she made a frantic effort to elude him and reach the open window. Her pitiful attempt to escape was in vain, though. He reached her before she could climb through it to safety.

Annie's resistance had only increased the killer's rage. He hacked at her until what was left of her small body was slumped down in a kneeling position, leaning against the open window. Her two sisters, seventeen-year-old Pearl and seven-year-old Rosebud, had fared no better. They already lay dead in their beds as Annie met her horrible end. They had been the first to be killed when the murderer rushed in. The only mercy spared them was that their killer had administered their deaths quickly.

With Annie's screams now silenced forever, all became deathly quiet in the farmhouse. The only living persons left in the house now were the two killers.

The sudden, heavy quiet in the death house brought Tom back to some kind of sanity. He had been in such a state of insane rage while slaughtering his family that his rational mind had shut down.

Now, dropping his axe, he looked with horror at the carnage around him. The attacks had been so brutal and vicious, there was blood, brain tissue, and gore all over the walls and beds in the three murder rooms. Even the ceilings were spattered with it. The floors themselves were slippery with blood. Tom's horror was not from guilt, though. It was from the fear of being found out. His partner, meanwhile, felt absolutely nothing. He had gotten his rush during the killings and now that feeling had passed.

The dilemma facing the two murderers now was that they had to come up with a plausible explanation that would throw suspicion off them.

Much to Tom's relief, the other killer appeared to have it all worked out. Tom was to profess his innocence and never deviate from this claim. He was to tell the authorities that the reason he was the only occupant of the house to survive was that he had managed to escape the killers by jumping out a window. His partner in the heinous crimes also told Tom to tell no one he had come to visit him that night.

"If you ever tell anyone I was here, I will have to tell them about your part. Then they'll know beyond a doubt that you're guilty," his murderous accomplice stated. "Remember, never admit your guilt and never tell them you know me."

By now it was getting on past four in the morning. The dawn of a bright, new day was well on its way for everyone except the slaughtered Woolfolk family innocents. Tom's partner told him to rush to the neighbors and act like he needed help. He was to tell them that his family was being murdered, and would they come back with him to drive the murderers away? The man said this would provide an alibi.

Tom's unstable, irrational mind gratefully accepted his partner's plan with no reservations. He didn't seem to realize that his fellow murderer was setting him up to take sole blame for the murders. The other man now took off, and Tom ran to the neighbor's house as planned. When Tom got there and woke them with his story, they refused to go back with him, though. The only thing left for him to do was to return by himself to the death house. Now he had no alibi and his treacherous accomplice was long gone, leaving him "holding the bag," so to speak.

He couldn't tell about his accomplice because people would know for sure he was guilty of the murders. What to do?

When he got back and lit a lamp, he realized with horror that he had gone to the neighbor's still wearing his blood-spattered clothing. Panic gripped him! Ripping off his blood-soaked clothes, he lit a lamp and tried to wash the blood off his body by its weak light. Knowing that people were on the way to see what had happened at the Woolfolk Homestead, Tom, with no time to find a better place, threw his bloody clothes into the well.

Sure enough, a short time later the neighbors showed up. It didn't take long before word spread around the nearby countryside about the horrible, grisly scenes at the Woolfolk farm. More and more people arrived, rumors spread. Needing some kind of order before things got out of hand, the sheriff was sent for.

Tom quickly became the focal point of suspicion. When questioned by the sheriff, his story didn't seem to add up. He nervously rambled on through his version of what had happened at the farmhouse. Instead of being numb with grief and shock over the gruesome murders of his family, he appeared edgy and apprehensive, immediately going on the defensive.

The neighbor Tom had gone to earlier asked him where his blood-spattered clothes were. Tom told him he had returned home, changed his clothes, and cleaned himself up as best he could. When asked where the blood on his clothes had come from, he claimed he had gone back in to check on the victims. While checking to see if any were still alive, he'd gotten blood on himself. Not satisfied with his explanation, the sheriff asked Tom once again where his blood-spattered clothes were. He claimed his state of shock over the murders had been so extreme, it had blocked out his memory of where he had left them.

As the sheriff questioned Tom, he noticed specks of dried blood in his ears and a bloody handprint on his leg. As if Tom's nervous, apprehensive manner and these observations weren't enough to raise doubts about his innocence, his short-handled axe, covered with blood and hair, was found in one of the murder rooms. Witnesses stated they had seen him using it the day before while making baskets. Then there was the inescapable fact that there was no forced entry or apparent burglary.

Still disturbed by the missing blood-soaked clothes, the sheriff sent men to look for them. They returned with them shortly, stating they had pulled them from the well. By this time, several hundred people had gathered at the Woolfolk farm. As more information was shared among the assembled citizenry and Tom's possible involvement, the crowd's mood shifted from curiosity to anger.

Things moved rapidly.

No time was wasted before a coroner's jury was hastily assembled right then and there. Based on the irrefutable circumstantial evidence, Tom was found guilty of the murders of his family.

The crowd was now primed and prepared to lynch Tom, but the sheriff's quick actions robbed them of this satisfaction. Sensing the crowd's mood, he had already arrested Tom and carried him off to jail.

The murders were such a sensation, the national press gave them extensive coverage over an extended period of time. When writing about the murders, the national press always referred to Tom as "Bloody Woolfolk," "fiend," "devil," and "monster."

As time passed, though, the uproar died down. Just when Tom thought he might be forgotten for a while in his jail cell, his trial came up, sparking the sensationalism all over again.

His first trial began on December 5, 1887. I say first because, even though Tom was found guilty on December 15, 1887, after the jury deliberated for all of twelve minutes, a second trial was ordered. This second trial was to make sure the defendant was being treated fairly. Doubts had been cast about the fairness of the first trial because, during the closing arguments, the spectators had become overexcited and rowdy, yelling, "Hang him! Hang him!" and the judge had done nothing to silence them.

Tom's second trial began on June 3, 1889. It lasted until June 24, 1889.

Unlike the first time, the jury deliberated a little longer, all of forty-five minutes, before delivering a guilty verdict.

Early the next morning, on June 25, Tom was sentenced to die on the gallows. As the sentencing judge proclaimed it, "to be hung by the neck until he is dead." Throughout both trials, he had continued to proclaim his innocence, but the overwhelming circumstantial evidence irrefutably contradicted his claim. Then, because Tom had claimed he was unable to describe the men he had escaped from, there was no one else to blame the murders on.

Now he understood the dilemma he had allowed himself to be trapped in by his devious fellow murderer. If he named his accomplice, the man would turn on him and confirm Tom's true role in the murders. Tom now knew that the murderous sharecropper had not only planned all along to destroy the Woolfolk family, but also Tom himself. He had just chosen a more cunning way to achieve Tom's destruction. First, he had used him as a tool to gain access to the family and use his help to destroy them. Then he had left Tom to face the grinding wheels of justice all by himself. What was Tom to do? The only thing he saw he could do was to keep his mouth shut except to profess his innocence, and hope for the best.

When it came time for him to go to trial, the courts tried him for only one of the nine murders, that of his father.

They figured that, being as how you can only hang a man once, and how Tom was so obviously the murderer, one conviction would do the job. Besides, there were eight other victims to ensure justice was done.

It's ironic, but this murder was the one Tom didn't commit. So he felt he was telling the truth when he said he was innocent of the crime he was charged with. His partner had been the one to kill his father while Tom had dispatched his hated stepmother. He didn't seem to realize, though, that he was still guilty because he had been an accessory to his father's murder, and what about his other victims?

Because of his illogical thinking, he was in denial about the dire nature of his true situation. He believed he was going to be absolved of his father's murder. This skewed reasoning demonstrated how much his ability, or lack of ability, to think rationally throughout his life had always been influenced by his confused, twisted mind.

This lifelong pattern of delusional thinking and mental illness should have brought up the question of what his mental state had been at the time of the murders. But Tom's possible insanity at the time he committed the crimes was never brought up or asked about at either trial.

Whatever the circumstances leading up to his journey to justice, society was going to make sure he didn't escape paying the ultimate price for his crimes. On the beautiful fall day of October 29, 1890, Tom was hung before a huge crowd of ten thousand people. It was not only the sensationalism of the crimes, though, that brought out this large number of spectators. Tom's execution was going to be one of the last legal public hangings in Georgia before they were made private affairs of the state. The Georgia General Assembly had been trying to abolish public executions for some time. In 1893, they finally succeeded in making public hangings illegal.

The crowds had come to be part of a passing spectacle. They came with high expectations of being well entertained. They were not to be disappointed. As many in the crowd snacked on opossum sandwiches, Tom, noose around his neck, was dropped through the trapdoor in the scaffold.

His death was neither painless nor quick. His executioner had either misjudged his weight or not fitted the noose properly around his neck. Whatever the cause, the drop didn't break his neck instantly as intended. He swung at the end of the rope for fifteen minutes, frantically kicking as he slowly choked to death.

This was the inglorious, gruesome end to the physical life of "Bloody Woolfolk," as Tom was called. Although it was the end of his physical body, what happened to the spirit that had once inhabited it? You guessed it! Tom's spirit chose not to leave the physical realm, even if he no longer possessed the physical body required to be a part of it. Instead of moving on, he took up residence as a ghost at the grave sites of his victims buried in Rose Hill Cemetery.

That's where I found him when I visited the cemetery one bright spring day. I love history, and I love cemeteries. Visiting a beautiful, historical old cemetery is a way for me to combine those two loves. It's always a bonus, then, when I find a ghost in one.

Such was the case when my good friend Marta Irvington and I arrived at Rose Hill Cemetery that day. As we drove through the entrance arch, all appeared quiet and peaceful. That is, until we reached the Woolfolk family plot. There, ranged around an old stone wall to the side of the grave sites, were five young ghosts.

Wanting to study the dynamics between the ghosts, I asked Marta to stop the car so I could observe the group for a few minutes. One of the ghosts was that of a slight young man, and the other four were children. The young adult male ghost was sitting on the wall with two of the ghost children, a boy and a girl, seated on his right. The fourth ghost child, that of a toddler, was playing on the ground at their feet. The fifth ghost child was a young girl of around ten.

The young ghost girl was standing in front of the male ghost earnestly talking to him as she beseechingly held out her arms. He was crying and appeared confused, unstable. One moment he was talking calmly to the young ghost girl, and the next he was yelling at her.

I decided to approach the ghost children to see if I could help them with whatever their dilemma was. I asked Marta if she would mind waiting while I checked the group out. Being used to my eccentricities, and my predilection for ghosts, she told me, "Not at all, Boo. I'll wait right here." And she did.

I might add that Marta is a compassionate person, whether it be for animals, children, or ghosts. She hates to see anyone or anything suffering when a little help might alleviate it.

Leaving Marta, I slowly walked toward the group of ghosts. It never paid to rush into an otherworldly experience without first getting an idea of who was involved and what was going on.

At the worst, the human could be putting themselves in danger if they weren't energetically prepared and protected. Being unprotected could leave you open and vulnerable to a Pandora's box of unpleasant influences. (And no, I'm not the "Oh my gosh I see evil demons everywhere, to battle!" type of drama queen. I tend to save my drama queen persona for much more mundane matters, such as being stuck in heavy traffic while running late for an appointment.)

The point is, it's wise to be prepared when working with other realms of existence. At the least, your sudden appearance could startle the ghost, and poof, off they go! How are you going to stop them? You can't, hence my hesitation to approach these confused young souls too quickly. Although they were aware of the living around them, they were not used to the living being aware of them.

As I approached, I realized from photos that the distraught young male spirit was none other than the ghost of the infamous Tom Woolfolk. The ghost children were his four youngest half-siblings in the Woolfolk family, Annie, Rosebud, Charlie, and Mattie the baby.

I said hello and then sat on the wall next to them. The younger ghosts greeted me back. Tom glanced over at me, sullenly noted my presence with not so much as a grunt, and then turned back to the young ghost girl. He regarded me as an unwelcome interloper and was determined to treat me as such.

Boo working with the young ghosts by the Woolfolk family graves

In contrast, the younger ghosts relaxed after a few moments in my calm presence—at least, as much as they were able to, what with Tom's brooding energy lying heavily around them. In fact, the air around us was saturated with his menacing, unstable presence.

I tried to engage the dour young male ghost, but he continued to ignore my overtures. Not so the children. They were happy to have someone to talk to. I listened as they told me about themselves, their happy, tight-knit family, and Tom. Their feelings for him swung back and forth between fear and a yearning to love him and have this love returned.

As Tom interacted with his young siblings, I could see why they were afraid of him. One moment he was bullying and menacing, the next remorseful and crying. This violent instability must have characterized the relationship between him and his fellow family members in their physical life together.

The children, from listening to their talk, were aware of the horrible events that had transpired as a result of this strife. Yet here they were, both perpetrator and victims, still together even in Death. But why was Tom still here?

The fear of being judged on the Other Side for his heinous acts could be one reason trapping him in the Ghost Realm.

And what about the ghost children? Why were they still here? They had no reason to fear being judged once they crossed over to the Other Side. They, unlike Tom, carried no shame that would make them feel unworthy. Unable to contain my curiosity and concern for their plight any longer, I asked them, "Why are you children still here as ghosts? Aren't you aware that you have passed out of the Earth Realm?"

"Yes, but Tom won't let us leave!" they exclaimed, glancing fearfully at him.

"Why are you keeping your siblings trapped in the Ghost Realm?" I asked him in a tone that brooked no refusal to answer.

At my tone, Tom looked over at me, acknowledging my presence for the first time. Sometimes firmness and directness are the best methods to use when working with a recalcitrant, confused ghost (as they are when working with some humans who are clueless about something).

Even so, he still hesitated before answering my query with "I'm protecting them."

Caught by surprise, I paused for a minute before asking, "What are you protecting them from?"

"I don't know. I just know I must keep them close to protect them from something bad."

Tom didn't realize in his confused state that he himself was the "bad thing" he was protecting them from. This misguided attempt on his part to protect the children was his unconscious way of trying to undo the horrible deaths he had inflicted on them.

Just as it had been in life, though, his even-now-unpredictable temperament still frightened them in death. Even as Tom and I continued talking, I could see him switching back and forth between the young man who could be nice, and someone who was violent and unstable, scarily unpredictable.

It was hard to keep up with the ghost's restless, edgy energy. One moment we would be talking lucidly, and the next Tom had tuned me out as he angrily ranted to himself in a paranoid state. The ghost obviously still had the nasty, mean streak he had possessed while alive.

But where was this uncontrollable nastiness and bizarre behavior coming from? Then my beloved main guide, Black Hawk, came to my rescue with the answer. The young man had been schizophrenic! Now I realized the true nature and magnitude of the mental illness Tom had suffered from while alive. It was also now easy to understand why the ghost exhibited a much more confused and separated-from-reality energy than what existence in the Ghost Realm usually engendered.

He had been this way in life, and he was still suffering from his mental illness in death. No wonder his family hadn't known what to do with him until it was too late. In the 1800s, mental illness was a source of shame. No one wanted to admit that it was in their family, because that would have reflected badly on the other family members.

Even if a mental illness was acknowledged, it was not well understood, so there was not a lot in the way of effective diagnosis and treatment.

But there was a lot in the way of shame, judgment, and cruelty directed at the mentally ill. You were considered inferior.

"He's crazy!" everyone had said of Tom, and that was that.

This was the atmosphere he had grown up in. There had been no help for him anywhere. He had had to deal with the mental illness, the scary voices, in the best way he could all by himself. As he had grown older, his mental condition had deteriorated. As it had grown worse and more out of control, so had his self-loathing.

He had known his erratic behavior brought him unwelcome attention and judgment, and he had blamed himself to a certain extent. He was supposed to be a man, able to handle anything, not a weakling.

Instead, as time went by, he had been less and less able to control the unstable, violent aspects of himself. The more often these episodes of schizophrenic paranoia and anger occurred, the stronger the self-loathing and disgust grew. This self-loathing made it harder and harder for him to accept and integrate his "bad self" into his whole being in a healthy way.

Therefore he had operated more and more from a state of denial of his true whole self. He'd thought that if he denied it enough, it would go away. Instead, the opposite had occurred. The more he had loathed and rejected "Bad Tom," the more this other aspect of himself had manifested. This other aspect was only trying to gain attention and acceptance in order to create a whole being. But there had been no one around to try and understand him and help him. He had been tortured by this struggle his whole physical life.

Now, in death, he still had found no surcease from this torment. As he had in life, he was still, in death, trying to deal with this darker side through harsh self-judgment and condemnation, instead of self-love and compassion.

Yes, Tom was definitely one confused, angry ghost!

I asked him, "Tom, are you aware of the crimes you committed when you were alive?"

He glared menacingly at me. "I'm innocent, I tell you. I'm innocent!"

"You don't remember committing heinous crimes against your family?"

"No, because I didn't do them!"

The exchange went back and forth like this between us for a time, with me confronting him and him denying any involvement in the murders of his family. I tried to strike a balance between being compassionate but also firm and determined the whole time. If he stayed in denial of his crimes, he would never face what he had done. If he didn't face them and accept responsibility, he wouldn't be able to work through them to find peace.

The ghost children, meanwhile, were staring at their older brother with wide, frightened eyes. It was obvious that before this time, they had never discussed their gruesome passings. Tom himself grew more and more agitated and upset with the path our conversation was taking. The energy emanating from him had become even more unsettled and edgy.

Knowing I wasn't getting anywhere with him by myself, I sent out a plea for help. The angels started assembling to help with the plight of the ghost siblings. Their loving, calming energy was felt immediately.

Baby Mattie crawled over to me and pulled herself up with a giggle to a wobbly standing position by clinging to my left leg (or rather, the etheric energy of my left leg). As she clung to my leg, I tried to ignore the intense cold created by the little baby ghost as she absorbed my warm energy.

The angels' energy had calmed Tom down enough to where I could once again ask him, "Tom, why did you kill your family?"

Once again, he started to respond with denial. Then, in midsentence of "I di—" he broke off and exclaimed in horror, "Oh my God, I did, I killed them!" In sudden anguish, the young male ghost broke down, sobbing over and over, "I didn't mean to do it, I didn't mean to do it!"

Moved by the ghost's anguish and emotional suffering, I told him I loved him.

"How can you love me? I'm wicked!" he sobbed.

"No, you're not," I quietly responded.

Seeing and feeling her brother's distress, gentle-hearted Annie closed the gap between them, putting her small arm around his neck in an attempt to comfort him.

"We forgive you, Tom. We love you," she gently told him.

Distraught now at her words and actions, he growled at her and pushed her away. Annie's compassion made him feel even more guilty and undeserving. Reading her brother's anguish and confusion correctly, she now wrapped both small arms around Tom's neck in a determined effort to comfort him. Once again, he tried to push her away, but I stopped him by saying, "Annie loves you, Tom. Don't reject her now as you did in life."

I knew the young ghost girl's touch, although painful for him, would act like a catharsis to help bring about his healing. Sure enough, at Annie's loving touch, Tom starting sobbing even harder as the memories from his now-lucid mind flooded his being. He was now face to face with the heinous crimes he had committed against his family. The accompanying guilt was almost more than he could bear.

He turned away from his siblings in deep shame. Quickly they gathered around him, exclaiming they loved him and forgave him. The children's affection for their big brother was obvious as they touched and caressed him with their small hands (something they had never dared in life).

Tom would have none of it, though, believing himself undeserving of such redemption. The depth of his anguish and sadness was almost overwhelming. I almost cried myself, but I couldn't give in to my emotions, because this would lower my vibrations and place me back in the Earth Realm. This would sever my energetic connection with the ghost children.

Silently, I composed myself.

Meanwhile, more and more angels gathered around us with their powerful, loving energy, filling the air with a soothing calm.

They were not the only source of this great peace, though. Another powerful presence was materializing in our midst.

The figure wore beautiful purple robes and had a glowing, golden aura all around her. I realized Mother Mary now stood in our midst. Her energy was so soft yet so powerful because of the strength of her goodness and grace. After all, she does have a special place in her heart for children and families.

She had come to give aid to Tom and his siblings, for it was time for this group of ghost children to decide. Would they go to the Other Side where the warmth of Divine Love awaited them? Or would they keep themselves trapped in the murky, cold realm of the Ghost Realm?

It was their choice. Their decision soon became obvious, though, as I observed the effect of Mother Mary's radiating, loving energy. They were gazing at her in wonder and awe as their young faces shone with the beginnings of hope.

A beautiful, loving smile lit up her serene face as she held out her arms, beckoning Tom and the children to her. With Annie carrying little Mattie in her arms, the ghost children ran with squeals of delight and excitement into Mother Mary's welcoming, protective embrace. The portal of golden Light leading to the Other Side opened behind her.

As she took baby Mattie into her arms, she gazed tenderly down at Annie, Charlie, and Rosebud as they clung to her. She now turned back to Tom, who had remained sitting on the cold, stone wall by the grave site, silently watching the scene.

With a smile full of tenderness, Mother Mary told him, "Come, Tom. Join us."

Looking wistfully at Mother Mary and the golden Light, he asked me, "Could this be for me also?"

"Yes, Tom, the Grace of the Other Side belongs to all, no matter what they've done in their earthly life. There's no judgment on the Other Side, only love. The Other Side is where you will find the peace and love and understanding that eluded you in your physical life. It's there that you will gain understanding as to why your life on earth followed the course it did."

By this time, Tom's brother and sisters were calling out to him in a chorus of "Come on, Tom! We love you, Tom! Come with us. Oh, do come with us, please!"

Despite their pleas, Tom still hesitated to go toward the Light.

I could hear the doubts and fears playing through his mind: *At the last moment, will I be rejected as I was in life? I'm not good enough. I'm a monster, everyone said so. Why should I deserve this?*

On and on the doubts ran, preying on his mind. Listening to him, I grew concerned that he was going to pass up this chance to free himself from the Ghost Realm, thereby missing the opportunity to find peace. A peace he had been seeking for so long. Was he about to prolong the waiting?

Just then, Mother Mary turned and handed Mattie back to Annie.

Turning back to Tom, she gave him the most radiant, loving smile as she held out her arms to him. "Come, my child," she gently told him. "It's your time."

He stood and walked toward her as if he feared she would turn from him in disgust at the last moment. Then, accepting that the Grace she offered was for him, he broke into a run and ran into her waiting arms.

As Mother Mary tenderly enfolded Tom in her arms, the most incredible energy of love, hope, and peace spread around us. I found myself crying, but now it was from the sheer joy of this Divine energy. Tom had finally found a safe haven.

Still holding him in her arms, Mother Mary asked him, "Are you ready to go Home now, my child?"

With newfound hope, he smiled and simply answered, "Yes."

As if waiting for that signal, the angels now gathered around Mother Mary, Tom, and the children to escort them on their journey to the Other Side. With Mary's arms enfolding them and angels all around, Tom and his siblings stepped into the Light and into the waiting arms of their parents.

Mother Mary turned and gave me a last beautiful, benevolent smile.

"Well done," it seemed to say.

Then she too turned back and passed through the portal of Light. The golden Light instantly closed and disappeared. I could go no further with them on their journey, but I knew all would be well with the Woolfolk family. For they were now truly a united family—united by love.

BUT HE PROMISED ME!

Dauphin Island, Alabama, is a small island located about three miles across Mobile Bay from Mobile, Alabama. It's approximately fourteen miles in length and a mile and a quarter wide. However, these dimensions are constantly fluctuating as a result of the severe storms that sweep through the area. The island has known continuous human occupation for at least fifteen hundred years, starting with the Mississippian culture of prehistoric Native American mound builders. The Mississippian culture lasted approximately from AD 800 to AD 1500. This prehistoric culture flourished in the eastern, southeastern, and midwestern portions of what is now the United States.

These early mound builders were either assimilated by or were the actual ancestral forerunners of modern tribes like the Choctaw, Chickasaw, Creeks, Cherokee, and Seminoles. Archeologists have never been able to prove their origins conclusively one way or the other. What is known, though, is that with the arrival of the first Europeans to the area of Dauphin Island and Mobile Bay in 1519, the permanent disruption and disintegration of the Mississippian culture began. This was the year the Spanish explorer Alonso Pineda arrived to map the island and the entire gulf coast of Florida for the Spanish crown. However, the Spanish didn't stay, as they were focused on developing their Florida territory.

This left the way open for the French to move into the area in 1699 with the arrival of the French explorers, led by Pierre Le Moyne d'Iberville. When the explorers arrived on Dauphin Island, imagine their shock and horror when they discovered a huge mound of human bones piled on top of one of the shell mounds. By their count, there were at least sixty skeletons, both male and female. They erroneously concluded that the island was the site of a massacre, and thus the name they bestowed on the island was set: Massacre Island.

Historians have since concluded that the French assumption was wrong. They offer two different conclusions. The first is that the bones were in a burial mound that was disturbed and raked open by a hurricane. The second conclusion is that the bones could be credited to the warfare that would break out among warring tribes for the rich bounty from the sea. The reputation of the abundant food resources to be found on the island and in the surrounding waters had traveled far and wide, bringing even tribes from far north into the area. If two tribes were friendly, they might be able to coexist while harvesting this bounty. If they were enemies and arrived at the same time, it could be a no-holds-barred fight when it was a matter of gathering food supplies to ensure survival in the coming winter months.

Whatever the origin of the pile of bones, it didn't deter the French from settling into the region. By 1701, they were entrenched in the Mobile Bay area. In 1704, because of its natural harbor, Massacre Island became a bustling port and the capital of the French Louisiana territory.

It was the perfect settlement for the French in every way except one: it lacked women. This distressing lack of female companionship for the settlers was remedied in 1704 by the arrival of the ship *Pelican*. On board were twenty-six young women sent by the king of France. As you can imagine in a colony comprised almost entirely of men, the *Pelican* girls, as they were called, had no trouble finding suitable husbands.

In 1707, it was deemed that the name Massacre Island was no longer appropriate for the busy port, so the name was changed to Isle Dauphine in honor of the wife of the heir to the French throne.

The French were unable to hold on to this important shipping port, though. As time passed, so did its ownership. Dauphin Island has had five flags flying over it. The first was the French flag. In 1764 the British, desirous of such a port in this part of the New World, captured the island. Then the Spanish seized it in 1780 while the British were preoccupied with the American Revolution. In 1813, the Americans took it from the Spanish to keep the British from using it in the War of 1812. To state it more accurately, the Americans were reclaiming territory that was already theirs. Dauphin Island had come to them when President Thomas Jefferson purchased the Louisiana Territory in 1803 for the sum of $75,000.

The fifth flag to fly over Dauphin Island was that of the Confederacy during the Civil War. After the Civil War, the island's citizens went about rebuilding their lives. Dauphin Island once again settled back into its relaxed rhythm. As the years came and went, nothing affected the island but the hurricanes. These could be severe at times.

The records of the island state that the 1906 and 1916 storms were so severe, people were forced to tie themselves to live oaks to keep from being swept away. Even the island livestock were not immune from the storms' fury. People tell of seeing the island's goats climbing onto the tree branches to escape the alligators and the flooding waters below.

As you can see, Dauphin Island, as well as its inhabitants, is resilient and tough. Despite this toughness, there's a graciousness and charm about the island and its people that are freely offered to its visitors. Today these visitors come for the island's beautiful beaches, history, and outstanding fishing.

The beautiful coastline is what drew me to Dauphin Island the first time I came. When I returned for the second time, it was for the history and the chance to investigate the ancient shell mounds on the island.

On my first visit to Dauphin Island, some of the local residents had told me the mounds were haunted. Now, some years later, I found myself standing at the entrance to Shell Mound Park. I thought about what I had been told earlier about the old mounds by residents who grew up here. One elderly lady had told me that her mother wouldn't let her go on the shell mounds after dark. Other parents also had this restriction for their children.

The reason for this prohibition seemed obvious to them: the mounds were haunted. When I asked her why they thought so, she told me that on quiet, dark nights you could sometimes hear the sound of Indian drums being played on the mounds. One man told me that people who had braved the mounds at night had seen spectral figures dancing in the moonlight, accompanied by drums. Another longtime resident told me that throughout the years people had heard crying and wailing coming from the woods on the mound.

Was this crying coming from a lost soul, or was it the ghosts of Indian women mourning their dead after a skirmish with the enemy? No one knows for sure, but one thing is certain: all is not quiet and peaceful on the ancient shell mounds.

But I was not here to investigate all of the mound's paranormal activity. I was here to try to help one lost soul, a ghost that my guides and angels had told me was trapped here. And so, accompanied by my intrepid friend Beth Sullivan, I found myself on the path leading to the mounds.

As we neared the mounds, the wind coming off of the Gulf started blowing strongly. The temperature plummeted. It was fall and the days were growing shorter. The late-afternoon sun was already starting its slide toward the western horizon.

I hurried up the side of the mound, for I knew I wouldn't have much time to locate the ghost before the bitter nighttime cold set in. As it was, we were in for an uncomfortable afternoon and early evening because of the weather. Beth was enjoying it no more than I. But a job is a job.

As we hurried toward the woods on top of the large shell mound, I realized there was one reason to rejoice over the bitter cold, one that I was truly grateful for. The island's large, aggressive mosquitos liked the cold wind no better than we did. They were in total abeyance for the night, which was lucky for Beth. Mosquitos tend to ignore me when other blood sources are available, but when they hone in on Beth, they tend to swarm her in legions in an attempt to carry her off. The mosquitos on this day were nowhere to be seen, though, or I should say felt?

I couldn't say as much for the freezing wind blowing off the Gulf. It blew constantly. We entered the woods and even there it followed us, blowing through the live-oak trees. The waning, weak afternoon sun couldn't shine through the live oaks, and so the woods took on a chill of their own. Massive clumps of gray Spanish moss hung in the gloom in large streamers from the branches, waving in the wind. Large, low-lying branches spread out horizontally from each tree. As is my habit when I see such massive, old trees, I wondered what scenes of life they had been witness to over the centuries.

*Magnificent, ancient live oak
on the shell mounds at Dauphin Island*

As I walked deeper into the woods, the chilly gloom steadily increased. I started to faintly pick up a presence moving in the shadows among the trees. This was the ghost my guides had told me about. I could see other spirits moving around the big shell mound, but she was the one I had come to find. I entered the deeper shadows under one large tree and sat down on one of its horizontal branches to wait for what was to follow.

It wasn't long before I saw the ghost herself slipping among the trees, moving closer and closer to me. As the entity drew near, I saw that it was the ghost of a young Indian girl. She couldn't have been more than thirteen years old. She was looking here and there as if she were searching for something. Around her was an aura of fear and desperation.

When I tuned in to her energy I could hear her wailing and crying, "Oh where is he, where is he?"

I realized she was searching for a man. The ghost moved closer to where I was sitting and then stopped about twelve feet away. She continued to look searchingly around, and then looked right at me.

Ah, she's aware of my presence! I thought.

I held my breath, waiting for her to acknowledge me. After a moment, though, I realized that this awareness of the other was a one-way street, for while I saw her, she was looking right through me as if I weren't there. I realized then the degree of her obsession with whatever had been her life issue at the time of her death. She had allowed it to trap her not only in the Ghost Realm, but also in a sort of time warp. She was trapped in time—a place in time that I was not a part of.

I would have to make her cognizant of my presence, though, if I was going to be of help to her. Because of the ghost girl's obvious timidity, I'd have to be careful not to frighten her while doing this. To startle her would ensure her disappearing into thin air.

With this in mind, I started gently sending her my energy. After a few minutes of standing there, though, the ghost turned away to continue her quest. I thought I had failed to gain her attention, but then something arrested her. She turned back toward me, looking right at me once again. All of a sudden, the ghost saw me!

Giving a startled gasp, she asked in alarm, "Who are you?"

For a moment I thought she was going to take off running, but she held her ground. Her need to enlist my help to find the man she searched for was greater than her fear of me. Neither of us moved as we studied the other, she more from curiosity of me than trust. While she looked at my strange clothes and pale hair and skin in wonder, I looked at her in dismay.

The young Indian girl was small of stature and her thin face was pinched from hunger. Her chest, arms, legs, and face were covered with bruises and open wounds, some of which still oozed blood. Her long, black hair was dull, dirty, and matted in places with this blood.

What happened to her to bring her to this state? I wondered in horror.

Her deerskin skirt, for that was all she wore, had once been a beautiful tan color, but now it was filthy and stained. Many sizes too large for the young girl, it hung on her thin, bony hips. It had been worn by many former owners before coming into the girl's possession. I suspected that underneath the skirt even more bruises and wounds covered her body.

She continued to study me as I sat quietly on the limb, giving her time to get used to my presence. I could hear her thinking, *Who's this being? Does it mean to hurt me?* Deciding I meant her no harm, she slowly approached me. Moving closer and closer to my perch, she stopped about six feet away, resting her small right hand on the bent trunk of the old live oak beside her.

Ah, she's giving herself room to run if she has to, I thought.

With the ghost girl's closer proximity, the air around me took on a thicker, heavier chill, a chill different from the ever-present cold of the evening. Now surrounded by her cold, I waited for her to speak.

The Indian girl continued to stand there, first staring at me and then down at the ill-fitting moccasins covering her small feet. I studied her back as one would observe a fawn; she was that young looking and delicately formed.

With the distance almost nonexistent between us now, I was able to see the beautiful child-woman she was. Even the dirty, shapeless deerskin skirt and horrible wounds could not mar her beauty.

Finally, I broke the silence between us by asking her name.

"I'm called Small Deer," she answered in almost a whisper. There was an air of deference around her as she spoke to me. She fell silent again, waiting to speak further.

What is she waiting for? I wondered. Then the realization hit me. Small Deer had been a slave. In life she had not been allowed to speak unless granted permission. "Small Deer, you can speak to me anytime you want to. You don't need my permission," I gently told her.

Despite her distrust of me and distress about her situation, her intelligent nature couldn't help but cause her to be curious about me. Her attention, at least for the moment, was arrested by the differences between my physical appearance and those of the people she was used to. I couldn't help but smile in amusement over how I must appear to her. Giving me a tentative, cautious smile, the young ghost started to relax.

"Who are you?" she asked.

"My name is Boo."

"What people are you from? I have never seen your people, because I have never seen anyone wearing clothes like yours. Where are you from? Are you a hunter? Do others of your kind have hair like yours?" She was now intently studying my long, blond hair as she waited for my answers.

"My people come from far away. Yes, there are many people with hair color like mine where I come from."

"Why are you here? Are you here to prepare for the coming time of cold?"

"No, I have come looking for you."

At my words I could feel her confusion grow. Yet with the approaching darkness possibly catching me in these unfamiliar woods, I didn't have time to explain too much. And so, directing her attention off of me and back to herself, I asked her, "For whom do you search?"

"My man, the father of my baby!" With these words she quickly crossed her thin arms across her abdomen, as if to protect something precious from a blow. Once again she looked at me, fearfully waiting for my reaction to her words.

Kindly I asked Small Deer to tell me about herself and how she came to be with child. Once again put at ease by my calm manner, she eagerly told me that she would soon have a husband. "He is going to marry me, and I will be free!" she exclaimed.

Her words now tumbled over themselves as she told me about the bright future she had planned for herself and her baby—a future that was no longer possible for her. It was too late; it didn't exist anymore. For her future, like her lover, would never come again to her, at least not in the Ghost Realm.

As I listened to the young ghost, I knew the time was approaching when I would have to try to help her understand that she was no longer physically alive. For now, though, I let Small Deer talk, telling me about herself and her earthly life. Not only was I genuinely interested in her as a spirit, but it would make it easier for me to help her cross if I understood what her entrapping issues were.

Boo helping young Indian ghost girl go into the Light

As Small Deer continued telling me about her plans for the future, she unconsciously moved over to my tree-trunk bench and sat beside me on the left. The temperature of the left side of my body dropped from the close proximity to the chill emanating from her form. As the cold grew stronger, I could feel her aura entering, permeating my living body's energy field.

She wasn't doing this to be mean or evil. In fact, she wasn't even aware that she was draining my energy. The cold around ghosts comes from their inability to manufacture energy on their own. When spirits walk through the Door of Death, they leave the energy-generating part of their whole form, the physical body, behind. When the spirit moves on to the Other Side, they then have access to unlimited energy because they're where the energy Source of everything is.

Whether she knew it or not during our exchange, Small Deer was using my life force, my energy, to help her stay active. I wasn't concerned about this, though, because I knew our encounter wasn't going to last for a prolonged period of time, such as when someone has a ghost in their house.

Now, in the heavy chill created by this young Indian ghost's proximity to me, I could see each breath I exhaled. I appeared to be the only one aware of my breath, though. She herself was oblivious to the fact that only one of us was exhibiting this vital validation of existence in the earthly realm, the breath of life. Because of her confused state, she was also unaware of the cold she was creating.

While I was noticing the chill, Small Deer's attention was drawn to my long, blond hair. My guides had told me to take it out of the ponytail I was wearing it in before I arrived at Shell Mound. When I asked them why, they told me it would help the young ghost feel more at ease by identifying with me in some way. It would also make it easier for me to engage her because of her curious nature. As always, my wise guides and angels were right.

The fact that my hair was long like hers did appear to be reassuring to her. Trustingly, the young ghost girl stretched out her small hand to feel my blond hair. "So soft, so soft..." she murmured, running her ghostly fingers through it.

Trying to ignore the distraction of the young Indian ghost's freezing aura, I asked her, "How did you meet your man, Small Deer?"

"Running Bear belongs to another tribe," she said with sparkling eyes. "His people, and the tribe of my masters, are harvesting the shellfish in preparation for the time of cold. I was at the water's edge one day cleaning the oysters with the other slaves and women of my village. He came down to wash his hands and arms after a hunting trip. He's a great hunter and will be a good provider for me and our baby.

"He was so handsome that I could not help staring at him. He noticed me then and beckoned me to him. I rose and tried to go to him, but the women prevented me by ordering me back to work. I dared not disobey, for to do so would bring a beating. I returned to my work but could not forget the smile he gave me as he turned and walked away.

" 'Oh, for a man such as that!' I thought. No one would dare beat me or make me go hungry as a punishment. He was not for me, though, as I was just a slave and unworthy. I tried to forget him.

"Later, I was in the forest gathering wood for the fires. I heard someone coming. When I looked up, it was he. As he approached, I put my head down and looked at the ground as I had been trained to do to my betters.

" 'Look at me,' he told me. When I did, he asked me, 'What is your name, little one?'

"I felt so shy, I could barely speak my name. 'Small Deer,' I whispered.

"He sat on the ground and motioned for me to sit in front of him. It was a great honor he gave me to let me sit with him. 'How old are you, Small Deer? How came you to be a slave?' he asked.

" 'I'm twelve or thirteen summers old. Yes, I'm a slave now, but I wasn't born a slave,' I told him proudly. 'I was five summers old when enemies of my people raided our village. I was asleep in my family's shelter. My people were taken by surprise. The people were running around screaming and crying. There was no way to escape. My father tried to protect us, but there were too many. He was killed by a war club as he ran out to fight.

" 'Some warriors ran in and tried to grab me and my mother. She got between them and me, trying to fight them off. A warrior thrust his spear through her breast. Her blood went all over me. I could not stop screaming. One of the men knocked me to the ground with a blow to the head. As I lay there, they bound my hands. I could struggle no more. It has been that way ever since. No use to struggle against my fate. I never saw my people again.'

"Running Bear seemed to understand my despair. He told me, 'Slavery doesn't have to be your life, Small Deer. Meet me here tomorrow and we will talk some more.'

"He was so kind to me. No one had shown me any kindness since I was taken from my village. I'm a nobody, a slave, deserving no better. This is how the people see me. I thought so of myself until Running Bear came into my life. How, then, could I refuse to meet him the next day when he asked me to? We have been meeting for many days now. He loves me and wants to make me his wife."

As she spoke, she smiled happily at me as she relived her memories of love, or at least what she had mistaken for love. The man had in fact cared nothing for the young slave. He had most cruelly abused her trust and deep longing for love and respect! Proof of this was that he had abandoned her and their unborn child to whatever fate awaited them.

As if she read my thoughts, which ghosts and most spirits on the Other Side can do, Small Deer gasped as she remembered her mission: finding her man. With this thought, Small Deer's happy smile disappeared as fear and desperation coursed through her being once again. Starting to cry, she turned to me, pleading, "Help me find him. We're in love and I'm to meet him here. I can't find him! His people are starting to break camp for their journey back to their land. I must find him!"

Her small hand gripped my arm in her agitated state, or at least she thought it did. The ghost girl was so upset, she was unaware that her hand was passing through my arm again and again as she tried to clasp it. "Help me, oh help me!" she begged.

"That's why I'm here, Small Deer, to help you," I assured her. "But I'm not here to help you find your man. He has already left to return to his home. I'm here to help you return to yours, your true Home."

"No, I must find him. My home is with him. Without him, I'm nothing!" she stated. Small Deer's words revealed how she'd let others define her and influence how she felt about herself. She had bought into the illusion that someone such as she, thought so inferior, had no right to happiness and joy. She had allowed her masters to break her not only in body, but also in spirit. She had had no control over how her body was treated, but she did have control over her spirit. The spirit was a part of her that was totally hers. As with any living person, no one could control or break Small Deer's spirit unless she allowed it. Small Deer had done just that.

She had given control over her personal spirit power to others. This had created the illusion of unworthiness she believed as true about herself when alive and even now in death. It was the illusion of not being worthy of love and happiness. This blocked her from accepting real love when it was hers for the taking—a love found not in the arms of a fickle lover, but found on the Other Side, where perfect love was available and abundant.

She would have to understand this difference in order to give up her obsessive mission to find this illusionary source of love, the false love of an unworthy man who had let her down. Once she understood and accepted this, she would be able to move on. It was time to be blunt with Small Deer.

"Small Deer, you're no longer alive in the earthly realm. Do you not realize you have died?" I asked her.

"No, this can't be!" she exclaimed in disbelief. "I carry his child. It will be a man-child and grow up to be a mighty warrior. Running Bear is a man of honor and has promised to look after me if I turn my back on the tribe that owns me."

"No, Small Deer, he is not coming back. He has already gone, leaving you to your fate. Do you not remember the day the women of your village learned of the child you were carrying? Look at your arms, your body. Don't you see the blood, the bruises?"

From the injuries on her body I had an idea of what had happened to Small Deer. But, wanting her to tell me about her death in her own words, I refrained from telling her my suspicions. I wanted the young Indian ghost girl to tell me herself for two reasons. The first was that it would verify what I was picking up by remote viewing into her past. When I do this remote viewing, I'm following the ghost's energetic trail psychically back to their last incarnation, lifetime, in the physical realm. The second reason I wanted Small Deer to revisit her death in her own words was that it would help her remember and accept the circumstances surrounding her death. This acceptance would help dispel her entrenched denial about her physical death. With this in mind, I once again prodded her, asking, "What of the bruises, Small Deer? How did you come by them?"

"What of these?" she impatiently asked. "I've been beaten many times and suffered many bruises from these beatings. When I was serving my master's food, if I dropped a piece of meat, he'd hit me in the face with the back of his hand. If my mistress or one of the other women became angry with me, I wasn't allowed to eat. If the food was all gone from the cooking pot before I was permitted to eat, I went hungry. There were many such days of hunger for me. I'm a slave, nothing more. It's how a slave is to be treated."

"But you're no longer a slave, Small Deer. You're no longer a part of that earthly realm, because you're dead. Death has freed you."

"How could I be dead? Today I'm supposed to meet my man and go away with him. He'll protect me and my baby." The young ghost was being quite resistant to accepting her demise. However, I understood that this resistance was coming from her great longing to have been loved and cherished while alive in the physical. It was hard for her to give up this great dream for the unknown territory of Death.

Little did the ghost realize, though, that the thing she'd been seeking throughout her life, unconditional love and acceptance, now awaited her on the Other Side with the Divine One and the angels. My time was growing short to convince her of this, though. Total darkness in the woods was approaching and the temperature was rapidly dropping. I would try once again to help Small Deer accept her true state of existence, for without this acceptance, she wouldn't be able to free herself from the Ghost Realm and move on. Again I asked her to tell me what she last remembered before she found herself in these woods looking for her lover.

"I remember going to the place where Running Bear said to meet him," she began. "He wasn't there. I searched and searched throughout the woods but I couldn't find him. I called and called his name but he didn't answer. I cried because I thought I had missed him. What will I do now, all by myself with a little one on the way?" The young ghost girl started sobbing in earnest as she remembered the fear and panic she had felt that day. She became so upset, in fact, it was hard for her to speak.

I prodded her to continue, though, telling her, "You're safe now, Small Deer. Do you not see these beings of Light standing around us? They'll keep you safe from harm."

The angels had assembled around us while we talked in preparation for escorting this lost soul Home. Small Deer looked around in wonder at the angels and the sparkling, golden glow created by their presence. Her sobbing ceased as the angelic energy calmed her agitated emotional state.

"Who are these beings?" she asked in a timid whisper of awe. "Where do they come from?"

"They're called angels. They're messengers from the Divine One, the being your people called Great Spirit. They bring unconditional love, joy, and peace. They're here to help you. But please continue your story, Small Deer. It's important that you do so."

With a long sigh, the ghost once again took up her sad tale. "I remember returning to the village after I couldn't find Running Bear. I ran to the place where his people were camped, but they were all gone. He'd left with them, leaving me and our baby behind. I was standing there crying as I looked out across the great water where my last hope had gone. I felt so alone and afraid . . . what was I to do?

"Then, from behind me, I heard shouting. When I turned, I saw the women from my village running toward me. Holding sticks and stones in their hands, they surrounded me. There was no escape. They angrily screamed at me that I had ruined their chance to sell me to another man by becoming pregnant. The man and his family now refused to buy me. My baby would mean another mouth for his family to feed.

"The women started throwing rocks at me and beating me with the sticks. I turned this way and that to avoid the rocks and sticks. There were too many, though. I was hit in the body, another hit my head. Then a rock hit me in the face, knocking me to the ground. Blood flowed into my eyes, blinding me. Although I couldn't see, I tried to crawl away. It did no good. The women were in a frenzy now.

"Once again I was knocked to the ground by their sticks. I curled up to protect my unborn child. They still beat me. After a while I felt no more pain from the blows. The women beat me till I knew no more. When I came to, I was lying on the ground all alone. The people had left, leaving me to fend for myself."

The young ghost girl had once again started sobbing as she recounted the events leading up to her death. With a startled gasp, she looked at me and exclaimed, "They left me behind because I was dead! I was dead! They didn't even think me worthy enough to dispose of my body properly. They left it to the wild animals!"

At long last, Small Deer's repressed memories had come flooding back. She'd been forced out of the physical realm, the realm of the living, and into that of Death by the fatal beating.

"What do I do now? Where do I go? Where do I belong? Am I still a slave?" Her questions now tumbled over each other in her confusion and agitation at the realization of her death.

"Did you never want someone to care for you, Small Deer, to not beat you and withhold food from you?" I asked in answer. "You're no longer of the earthly realm. Therefore, you don't have to stay in the life of a slave."

"What of my body?"

"Even though they didn't dispose of it, it still returned to where it belonged, to Mother Earth. The part of you that remains is the most important part, your eternal spirit. As such, it's time for you to go where you belong, to the Other Side to be with the Great Spirit."

The angels, with their infinite patience and love, were standing all around us now, waiting for the young Indian ghost to make her decision. Although Small Deer had possessed little free will in the physical realm because of her slavery, she now had total free will in that of the spirit. The golden Light, the doorway to the Other Side, now stood wide open, awaiting her. I could see Small Deer's loved ones gathering at the entrance to escort her Home.

For some reason, though, the young Indian ghost still hesitated to enter the Light. Then, with her next words, it became clear why. "What of my baby? Will I be able to see my baby?"

"Yes, but to do so you'll have to leave this place of sorrow where you have kept yourself trapped. Your baby is with the angels and is fine. He's waiting for you even now. Once you cross over, you become free. You're free to go wherever you want to and be whoever you want to be."

"If I go, will my masters come after me and punish me? I need a man to protect me!"

"You don't need a man to protect you now," I assured her. "No one can punish you ever again. You're all powerful because you're in your Divine spirit form. There's nothing more powerful. As for a man to claim you, do you not see the man standing there by the golden Light? Do you see the Light, Small Deer? Do you see the man?"

She looked. "Yes, it looks like my father from when I was a little girl living with my people. Why is he here?"

"He has come to take you Home to the Other Side. On the Other Side you will find your baby, love, freedom, happiness, all the food you can eat—everything that was denied you in your physical life. All the people you loved in your earthly life will be there to welcome you Home. All you have to do is take your father's hand, hold it, and go with him into the Light. He and the angels will look after you on your journey Home. You will arrive into the life you always dreamed of having."

Small Deer's face lit up with excitement at the acceptance of all that awaited her. She stood and started hurriedly walking, then running into her father's arms. He smiled down at her as he held her tightly to him. Then, with a "Welcome home, child!" he clasped her left hand, turned, and led her into the Light. But just before they entered, Small Deer paused, turned back, and gave me a beautiful smile. Holding her right arm toward me, palm facing out, she joyfully said, "Go in peace, Lightskin, as I go!"

Then she turned back to the Light and was gone. It was time for me to leave also, for the woods around me were now dark and cold. I had nothing to fear, though, for the myriad of stars shining above in the Universe warmed and reassured me and showed me the way.

CLOSING THOUGHTS

Dear readers,

    Before we go our separate ways, I would like to first offer my sincere thanks for coming on this journey with me and the ghosts in *Between the Realms*. From this book, it is my hope your perspective of ghosts has widened. Ghosts—and our understanding thereof—can teach us many things. Through the realization that they were once human beings too, with all the hopes, dreams, issues, frailties, and strengths that entails, we can better understand that it is by dealing with our issues in an honest, forthright way that we can grow and evolve. Ghosts teach us that we cannot run from who we are. We can only face ourselves with love and compassion and strive to grow.

    Ghosts also remind us that life goes on and on and on into eternity and beyond. Life does not stop with the end of physical life. Our energetic beings just change forms; they never disappear. We are, as Divine spirits, integral and interwoven into the cosmic scheme of the Universe.

                      I wish you happy, joyful journeying!
                                         Boo

ADDITIONAL RESOURCES

Old Decatur Cemetery
229 Bell Street
Decatur, GA 30030

Cemetery Operations: (404) 378-4411

The cemetery grounds are open to the public seven days a week. The cemetery is closed after dark. The police actively patrol the cemetery to protect it from vandalism.

Chickamauga and Chattanooga National Military Park
3370 Lafayette Road
Fort Oglethorpe, GA 30742

Chickamauga Battlefield Visitor Center: (706) 866-9241
Open daily from 8:30 a.m.–5:00 p.m.

The battlefield is open from 6:00 a.m. until sunset.

Old Cahawba Archaeological Site
9518 Cahaba Road
Orrville, AL 36767

Visitor Center: (334) 872-8058
Open Thursday–Sunday 12:00–5:00 p.m.

The park is open daily from 9:00 a.m.–5:00 p.m. Visitors are not allowed in Cahawba after dark unless participating in scheduled programs.

Rumble Seat Inn Bed and Breakfast
303 Forsyth Street
Barnesville, GA 30204

(770) 358-9348

Redcliffe Plantation State Historic Site
181 Redcliffe Road
Beech Island, SC 29842

(803) 827-1473

Park admission is free.
The grounds are open from 9:00 a.m.–6:00 p.m. daily.

House tours cost $7.50
House tour hours: Thursday–Monday, 11:00 a.m., 1:00 p.m., 3:00 p.m.

Indian Shell Mound Park
830 Desoto Drive
Dauphin Island, AL 36528

There is no phone number.
Open to the public from dawn to dusk.

Rose Hill Cemetery
1071 Riverside Drive
Macon, GA 31201

(478) 751-9119

Cape San Blas Lighthouse
200 Miss Zola's Drive
Port St. Joe, FL 32456

Lighthouse hours vary, so call (850) 229-1151 or (850) 229-8261.

Please be respectful of the grounds, artifacts, and hours of operation at the locations. Remember, their history is everybody's history!

BIBLIOGRAPHY

Adair, James. *The History of the American Indians*. London, 1775.

"Dauphin Island, Alabama." *Wikipedia*. Last modified June 8, 2017. https://en.wikipedia.org/wiki/Dauphin_Island,_Alabama.

Federal Writers' Project of the Work Projects Administration for the State of Tennessee. *Tennessee: A Guide to the State*. American Guide Series. N.p.: New Deal Network, 1996. Originally published 1939 by Tennessee Department of Conservation, Division of Information.

Granato, Sherri. *Haunted America & Other Paranormal Travels*. Bloomington, IN: LifeRich Publishing, 2015.

Mails, Thomas E. *The Cherokee People: The Story of the Cherokees from Earliest Origins to Contemporary Times*. New York: Marlowe & Company, 1996.

Mayhew, Henry. *Voices of the Poor: Selections from the* Morning Chronicle *'Labour and the Poor' (1849–1850)*. Edited by Anne Humphreys. Cass Library of Victorian Times 10. Abingdon, UK: Routledge, 1971.

National Park Service. "Chickamauga Battlefield." Chickamauga & Chattanooga National Military Park. Accessed June 13, 2017. https://www.nps.gov/chch/learn/historyculture/chickamauga-battlefield.htm.

Preston, Samuel H. and Michael R. Haines. *Fatal Years: Child Mortality in Late Nineteenth-Century America*. Princeton, NJ: Princeton University Press, 1991.

Watkins, Alfred. *The Old Straight Track: Its Mounds, Beacons, Moats, Sites and Mark Stones*. London: Methuen & Co., 1925.

Young, Frances, compiler. "A History of Dauphin Island Under Five Flags 1699–1989." Dauphin Island Foundation. Accessed June 13, 2017. http://difoundation.org/history.htm.

ABOUT THE AUTHOR

Boo Newell has been a practicing professional psychic medium for eighteen years. She is an acclaimed psychic, medium, spiritual counselor, paranormal investigator, and animal communicator. She is also a much-sought-after lecturer and teacher of the spiritual/metaphysical. Although she is based in Atlanta, Georgia, she has a loyal national and international clientele.

Born in Daytona Beach, Florida, she has been able to see and talk to ghosts and other spirits from the time she was a little girl. At first she was afraid of them, but as she grew up and gained understanding about the world of spirits, she became more comfortable with her psychic abilities and ghostly acquaintances.

Not only is Boo a professional psychic medium, she is also the owner and main tour guide of the highly rated Decatur Ghost Tour in Decatur, Georgia. The tour gives Boo an opportunity to combine two of her great loves: history and the paranormal. Working with the customers on the tour gives Boo the opportunity to expose them to the world of spirits and help them gain a greater understanding of this often misunderstood alternate realm.

For more information about Boo and her work, please visit her website at www. boonewell.com.